D1087456

Stories from the

# Bible

*Retold by Heinz Janisch*
*Illustrated by Lisbeth Zwerger*

*With notes and afterword*
*by Mathias Jeschke*
*Translated by David Henry Wilson*

North
South

## OLD TESTAMENT

NEW TESTAMENT

# OLD TESTAMENT

# THE CREATION OF THE WORLD

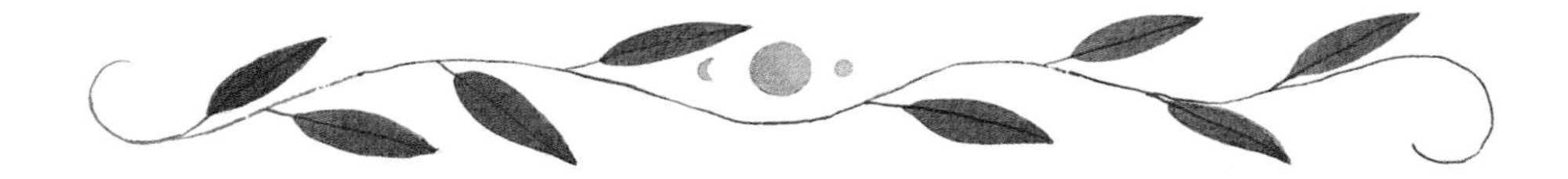

IN THE BEGINNING WAS THE WORD, and the Word was with God. The earth was still without a name; it was barren and empty and covered with dark water. Then God said, "Let there be light," and light appeared above the dark water. God separated the light from the darkness, and he called the light day, and the darkness night. This was the first day.

Evening came, and morning came.

God looked at the water and the bright light above it. He said, "Sky." And so he created the sky, an arch high above the water, so that he could say that one was below and one was above. This was the second day.

Evening came, and morning came.

God looked at the endless expanse of water before his eyes. He said, "Land." And sand and earth, stones and rocks came into view, providing barriers to keep the water within bounds. God called the dry land the earth and the watery waves the sea.

God took a long look at the earth.

"I want to see living green things here," he said. "Flowers and trees and plants of all kinds should grow and blossom and smell sweet!" And so there was sweet-smelling greenery everywhere, and flowers and blossoms delighted his eyes. God knew that it was good. This was the third day.

Evening came, and morning came.

God looked at what he had created so far. "The earth is decorated with shining flowers," he said. "But the sky should also be decorated." And so he created the sparkling stars and the moon for the night, and the sun for the day, to provide light and heat. This was the fourth day.

Evening came, and morning came.

God dipped his hand in the water and said, "I want to see living things here." And so he created fish and shrimps and mussels and everything that is able to live under the water.
God raised his hand high in the air and said, "I want to see living things here as well." And so he created birds and insects and all the flying creatures that can live in the air. This was the fifth day.

Evening came, and morning came.

God looked at the life in the water and in the air. "I want to see animals that run over the earth, that crawl on it and live in it; the earth should also be a home for lots of living things." And so God created all kinds of animals to live on the land.

He looked at everything he had created, and when he saw his reflection in the water, he said, "Now we will make human beings. They are to be like me, but they will live among the animals and plants and will be as beautiful and as fragile as they are." God took a handful of earth and created human beings as man and woman. He gave them both the breath of life and named the man Adam and the woman Eve. Then he blessed them and said, "Be fertile and have many children. This is your earth. Live in peace." This was the sixth day.

Evening came, and morning came.

The next day, God knew that his work was finished. He looked around and saw that everything was good. "Today I shall have a rest," said God the Creator. He blessed the day and made the sunbeams shine brightly. This was the seventh day.

That is how God created the sky and the earth, the animals, plants, and humans, and everything else that lives.

Evening came, and morning came.

# PARADISE

GOD HAD MADE THE SKY AND THE EARTH, above and below. He had created day and night, light and darkness. He could see the birds and clouds in the sky, and the flowers and grasses on the earth. There was life everywhere, but the fields were still bare and covered with dust. They were waiting for rain. The dust glittered in the light.

God looked at Adam and Eve, and he was pleased with them. They were naked, but they were not embarrassed, either before God or before each other.

Everything was new, and everything was bright and simple. "I'd like to create a nice place for all of us," said God. "I'm going to design a garden." He made trees grow out of the bare soil. Trees large and small, mighty and delicate, bushy and slender, stretched their branches up toward the sky.
God made a river spring from the earth, and he divided it into four streams. With these he could provide the garden with enough water for the trees and their roots and for everything else that he wanted to grow there. A warm and gentle breeze wafted through the air, rustling the leaves on the branches. Delicious fruits grew on the trees. They looked tempting, and each fruit was of a different shape and color.

God was pleased when he saw the garden, which he called Eden. He brought the animals he had created and showed them to Adam and Eve.

"It is not good for humans to be alone," he said. "Here are many animals that I have created. They are different from you, and yet they are living creatures just like yourselves. They live on the earth, in the water or in the air. Give them whatever names you like, and live side by side with them in peace."
And so God created a bond between the animals and the humans.

God took the humans to two trees in the middle of the great garden. One was the Tree of Life, with roots deep in the earth and branches that touched the sky. The other was the Tree of Knowledge. Red apples hung enticingly from its branches.
"You may eat all the fruits in this garden," God said to the humans. "But you may not eat the fruit of the Tree of Knowledge. This fruit would open your eyes to everything that is good and bad. Stay away from it."

The snake had heard God's words. "Don't you want to know what awaits you if you eat the forbidden fruit?" the snake asked Eve, who with much curiosity kept returning to the Tree of Knowledge.
One day, Eve could no longer resist her desire. She plucked an apple from the Tree of Knowledge and ate it. She also gave Adam a piece. When Adam and Eve had eaten the fruit, they saw the world in a different way. Suddenly they were embarrassed by their nakedness. They quickly covered themselves with fig leaves. They hid from each other—and from God. For the first time they had feelings of shame and fear.

Then in the cool breeze of the day they heard God's heavy footsteps. "Where are you, Adam?" asked God, although he had seen all that had happened. What he really meant was: "Why are you hiding from me?" Adam ducked down behind a bush, but he knew very well that it could not protect him.

He stepped out before God, even more naked than before despite the fig leaves, and Eve came and stood by his side.
God was very angry. First he turned to the snake. "From now on, you will have to make your way in the dust," he said to the snake. "You shall crawl on your stomach, day in and day out, and humans will be afraid to come near you. Out of my sight!"
Then he turned his gaze on Adam and Eve. "You have eaten from the tree whose fruits I forbade you to eat!" said God. "I made you out of dust and earth. The soil is cursed because of you! Every day of your life you will have to work hard to get your food. From now on thorns and thistles will grow in the fields among the plants that are meant to feed you. The sweat will pour from your brow as you cultivate the grain for your daily bread and harvest the fruit you live on. With your hands you will till the land until you return to the earth from which you came. For you were dust, and dust you will be again."

A cold gust of wind blew over Adam and Eve.
"You have eaten from the Tree of Knowledge," said God. "Now you know what is good and what is bad. Work the soil from which you came, and learn to live with joy and pain, with sadness and with hope."

God made clothes of warm fur for Adam and Eve. And then they had to leave the Garden of Eden.
East of Eden, God placed the cherubim, mighty angels carrying flaming swords. They were to guard the way to the Tree of Life forever. God had driven Adam and Eve out of the Garden of Eden because they had not obeyed his instructions. And so they went away, hand in hand, along the path to which God had directed them.

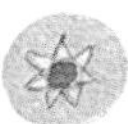

*The first two chapters combine two texts that can be found in the first few pages of the Bible. These are the two versions of the Creation. In poetic style they tell us how this world may have come into existence. Their focus, however, is on the origin of all things. The basic point of both texts is that there is a God who gave life to the world and all the creatures in it, and saw that what he had made was good.*

*God gave freedom to his creations. However, that also gave them the ability to turn away from him. This is what happens in the account of the events that took place in the Garden of Eden and—in the following chapter—with the story of Cain and Abel.*

# CAIN AND ABEL

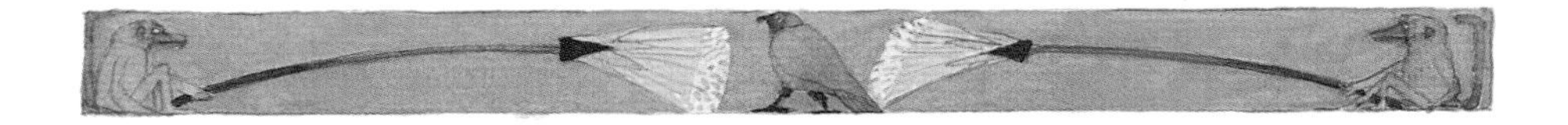

ADAM AND EVE HAD LEFT PARADISE. A hut to live in, a barren field, a flock of sheep—this was their new home now.

Eve gave birth to two sons, Cain and Abel. Abel was a shepherd, and Cain cultivated the land. Adam and Eve had told them all about God and Paradise, and so from time to time the brothers gave God a present: they roasted a nice piece of mutton in his honor, or placed a bowl of fresh fruit on a homemade altar. This was their way of asking God to protect them.

But Cain became more and more jealous of his brother. Had God been more pleased with Abel's presents than with his own? Were his parents' hearts more open to Abel than to him, the elder son? Such thoughts darkened his mind. More and more frequently, Cain went out into the fields with his eyes cast down.

God saw Cain's dark gaze and said, "Why are you so angry? Why do you scarcely dare to raise your eyes? Can you feel the jealousy poisoning your heart? Are you afraid that it can be seen in your eyes? Beware of your anger! You must master your rage or else it will take control of you!"

But Cain had already lost the battle against his anger. Secretly he made a plan. He took his brother Abel out into the fields to show him the harvest. But when they reached the fields, Cain picked up a large stone and killed his brother with it.

Just as God in Paradise had asked where Adam was, that evening he asked Cain about his brother. "Where is Abel?" asked God when Cain returned home alone. "Where is your brother?"

"I don't know," Cain answered sullenly. "Am I my brother's keeper?" God raised his voice. "What have you done? Your brother's blood cries out to me from the soil! I see the blood on your hands, and I see the blood on the soil. This earth will give you no more food because you have watered it with your brother's blood. You will have no rest upon this earth but will flee from yourself, an outcast, a wanderer who will never find a home."

Cain hid his face in his hands. He wept bitter tears. What had he done? "You must leave here," said God. However, he put a sign on Cain's forehead to prevent people from killing the outcast. That very night Cain left the land of his parents.

*God puts Cain under his protection, but in the story of the Flood he finally seems to have lost patience with humans. He decides to start things all over again, because humans have forfeited their right to life. But he makes a new agreement with Noah, his family, and all the animals and saves them from the Great Flood. When they finally set foot on dry land again, the rainbow becomes a sign of God's infinite mercy and endless love, which will shape the whole history of life on Earth.*

# THE GREAT FLOOD

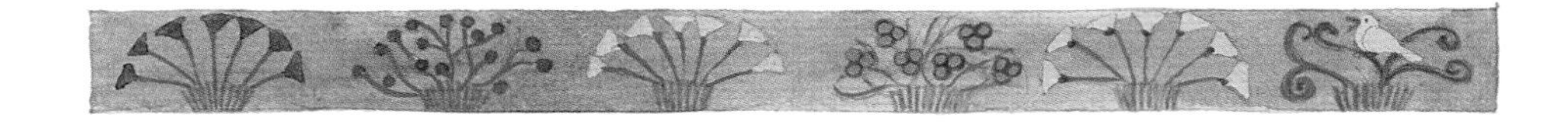

CAIN, WHO HAD MURDERED HIS BROTHER, had done a wicked deed. And soon people turned more and more in the direction of evil. Their thoughts, plans, and actions were increasingly aimed more at harming than at helping others. And they had also become cruel in their dealings with nature and with animals.

God was filled with anger. He was sorry that he had created humans. Their deeds hurt him to the very depths of his soul.

"I shall send a great rain," said God at last. "A terrible flood will remove from the earth all the humans whom I have created, and with them all the animals of the land and all the birds of the sky."

God looked around once more. The world was full of violence and evil. Only one man found grace in his eyes. That was Noah, who trusted in God and had brought up his three sons to do good to others.

God said to Noah, "I am going to cover the earth with a great flood. Go and build an ark, a ship of solid cypress wood that can withstand all winds and weather. Seal the inside and outside of the ark with pitch, so that it will be waterproof. The ark should be 150 meters long, 25 meters wide, and 15 meters high. Give it a roof over the top, and two decks in between so that it will have three stories. Then put a large door in the side.

"I shall send rain that will last for forty days. Everything that has not found refuge on the ark will be destroyed. But I will make a bond with you. You and your family will survive. After the flood, you will start a new life on earth. Take your wife, your sons, and your sons' wives with you on the ark. And take one pair, male and female, of every animal in the world on board, so that they may be saved. Think of all the animals that live on the land or in the air. Those that live in the water will not need the ark. Take with you food for all the animals and for yourself and your family. It will be a long journey."
Noah did exactly as God told him. He built a huge ark of cypress wood with many compartments. When it was ready, God said, "Go to the ark now with your family, and open the door wide so that the animals can find their places on your ship."

The animals had heard of Noah's ark. They came from all over the world to join him. Soon a long procession of animals was making its way into the ark. It took seven days and seven nights before they were all on board.

After Noah carefully sealed the entrance to the ark, the rain began to fall. For forty days it rained without stopping. The water rose all around, and slowly lifted the ark up high. It rained and rained, and the ark rose ever higher until it was floating freely on the water. Up and up climbed the flood, until finally even the mountains were covered with water. It stood seven meters above the highest peaks.
Everything that had lived now sank beneath the water, in accordance with God's wishes. The Great Flood destroyed all life on earth. Only Noah and those who had found refuge with him on the ark survived.

The days and nights on board the ark seemed endlessly long. The animals sat, stood, or lay close together in the belly of the ship, and Noah and his family spent all their time looking after them. They were hardly able to sleep. They went anxiously up and down the rows of animals, talking to them, stroking their fur, listening to their complaints, calming them, and distributing the food. Everyone waited in the belly of the ark, like children in the belly of the mother, waiting to be born.

At last the rain stopped falling. God sent strong winds to drive the waters apart and make them drain away. The peaks of the mountains became

visible. With a sudden jolt, the ark came to rest on top of Mount Ararat. The jolt was a shock to everyone on board, but nobody was injured.

Noah waited forty more days. The animals in the ark became very restless because they wanted to leave. But the Great Flood had made Noah cautious. He opened a small window and sent out a raven to explore the surroundings. The raven flew and flew, but all it found was an endless expanse of water. It returned, exhausted, to the ark.

Noah waited for a few more days and then sent out a dove to see if the water had finally drained away from the earth. But the dove could not find a single spot where it could land. The whole world was still covered with water. The dove also returned to the ark exhausted. And so the animals had to wait another seven days before Noah sent the dove out again.
When the dove returned with an olive leaf in its beak, Noah knew that at last the water had drained away. He waited another seven days, and sent the dove out once more. This time it did not return.

With great relief, Noah looked out the window and blinked in the sunshine. Then God said to him, "The Great Flood has ended. Take your family and all the animals out of the ark and enter the new world. Be fertile and have many children. But take good care of this earth. Be patient with yourselves and with others. Always remember that many things in this world have two sides: sowing and harvesting, cold and hot, summer and winter, day and night . . ."

Noah opened the large door and all the animals rushed joyfully out into the open air. God blessed Noah and his family and the animals too. "I shall never again send a flood to destroy the earth," said God. "And as a sign of this agreement between us, I shall make a rainbow in the sky.

That will remind you of the great rains and of the light, and it will bind what is below with what is above."

A rainbow appeared in the sky then. It bound together the earth and the sky. And this huge and radiant bow arched above them in bright and shining colors.

# THE TOWER OF BABEL

NOAH AND HIS DESCENDANTS became farmers. They looked after their fields and animals, and they planted vineyards. Soon people began to do all kinds of different things, and they became more and more inventive.

"We could take lumps of clay and bake them into bricks," some people said, and they started work at once.

"With baked bricks and stones and pitch we could build a town," said others, and they designed the first buildings.

"We could build the biggest tower the world has ever seen," said others, looking upward. "The tower should be so tall that it touches the sky."

In those days, there was only one language, and everyone understood what everyone else was saying.

The people discussed their plans, and very soon they began to build a town and a huge tower.

God saw the humans working day and night building their town and, brick by brick, raising the tower higher and higher into the sky. They were obsessed with the desire to create a building that would rise above all other buildings and make them famous.

"We shall be remembered forever because of this tower," they said,

and their eyes shone with excitement. "We shall be as great as God!" they cried.

Their vanity and pride made God angry. He decided to put an end to such arrogance, and so he made them all speak in different languages. No one could understand what anyone else was saying, and at once there was chaos and confusion. Later the town was called Babel.

Now the people began to quarrel. All those who spoke the same language formed groups, and they each thought their group was better than the other. There was no longer one single community, and so the people stopped building the town and the tower.

The quarrels between the groups became more and more violent, and very soon all the people left the town. Their houses stood empty and the tower that was supposed to touch the sky stayed half finished.

The men and women of Babel, the town of many languages, scattered in all directions, and they took their new languages to all corners of the earth.

*The story of the Tower of Babel describes how humans challenge God. By joining forces they hope to become so powerful that they can compare themselves to God and gain fame and fortune.*
*Their plan misfires. God once more puts humans in their place and divides them by making them speak many different languages. This state of confusion is resolved symbolically in the New Testament account of the miracle of Pentecost, which anticipates God's plan for salvation.*

# JOSEPH AND HIS BROTHERS

JOSEPH AND HIS ELEVEN BROTHERS lived with their parents in the land of Canaan. Joseph was much younger than his brothers, and perhaps that is why his father, Jacob, loved him more than the rest. He even had a special coat made for him in many different colors.

Joseph often had dreams. While he was asleep, he would see strange images and be told strange stories that were difficult to understand. He liked to tell his father and brothers about his dreams. Once he even dreamed that the sun, moon, and eleven stars bowed down before him.

Such dreams made his brothers angry, and they became more and more jealous. Did not this latest dream mean that Joseph saw himself as King, rising above them and even the sun, moon, and stars? Their anger increased day by day, until it became uncontrollable.

One day, when Joseph accompanied his brothers to the field, they tore off his clothes, including his multicolored coat, and threw him into a deep, dried-up well.

When they saw a group of merchants riding by on their camels, the brothers hatched a new plan. They pulled Joseph out of the well and sold him to the merchants for twenty pieces of silver. Now he could go

and be a servant in some distant country, far away from their parents' house!
They smeared Joseph's coat with the blood of a dead goat, and took it to Jacob, their father. They told him that a wild animal had attacked their brother in the fields and killed him.

Their father was heartbroken at this news. Was Joseph, his beloved son, really dead? In his grief, Jacob tore his own clothes to pieces and went into mourning. Something inside him had also died, and from this moment on, he grieved for his son and nothing could comfort him.

*The tale of Joseph provides a transition from the stories of the patriarchs—Abraham, Isaac and Jacob—to the history of a nation, which focuses on the people of Israel.*
*The brothers' intentions toward Joseph are not good. In their jealousy, they hatch a treacherous plan—initially to kill him, though subsequently one of them persuades the rest to sell him. The course of events leads to a situation in which Joseph can finally say to his brothers: "You had bad intentions, but God made something good come out of them by bringing me here. I shall go on looking after you and your children."*

# PHARAOH'S DREAM

THE MERCHANTS SOLD JOSEPH to Pharaoh's chief bodyguard, and so he ended up in Egypt. God was still by his side in Egypt, and Joseph was successful in all that he did. Although he was a servant, he was much loved, and very soon he was put in charge of the whole house. But one day the wife of the bodyguard made false accusations against him, and as a result Joseph was thrown into prison.

At that time Pharaoh's baker and cupbearer were both imprisoned with him for a few days. They had each done something to offend Pharaoh. While they were in prison, the baker and the cupbearer had strange dreams, and when they told Joseph about the dreams, he was able to interpret them.

One night Pharaoh himself, the ruler of Egypt, also had a dream that worried him. He was standing beside the River Nile when seven well-fed cows came out of the water and started eating the grass on the bank. They were followed by seven very thin cows that came out of the water, attacked the fat cows, and ate them.

Pharaoh sat up in bed, his face pale with fear. What could this strange dream possibly mean?

He lay down again and tossed and turned until once more he fell into a deep sleep. Then he had another dream. Seven ears of grain grew on one stalk, and they were full and fine. But now from the same stalk grew seven ears that were thin and withered, and the seven thin ears swallowed up the seven fat ears.
Pharaoh woke up and sent for his fortune-tellers and dream-interpreters, but none of them knew the meaning of the dreams.

Then the cupbearer, who had now been let out of prison, remembered Joseph, and he remembered how well Joseph had understood the language of dreams. He told Pharaoh, who had Joseph released from prison and brought before him. Pharaoh told Joseph about the two dreams.

Joseph bowed to Pharaoh and said, "My Lord, the two dreams mean one and the same thing. The seven fat cows and the seven full ears are seven years during which your land will have plenty. The seven thin cows and the seven withered ears are seven years in which there will be a terrible famine. After seven years of abundance, the land will suffer from seven years of drought, and so the seven fat years will be followed by seven lean years."

Pharaoh thanked Joseph for his explanation. Then Joseph said he knew what had to be done. Corn from the seven good years should be collected and put in large stores so that during the seven years of drought and famine no one in the land would need to go hungry.
Pharaoh agreed. He praised Joseph for his wisdom and made him his chief counselor and representative. Soon Joseph was famous all over the country. Pharaoh himself and many of the mightiest lords bowed before him, just as the sun and moon had once done in his earlier dream.

Everything came to pass exactly as Joseph had said it would. For seven years there was an abundance of food. On behalf of Pharaoh, Joseph traveled all around Egypt gathering corn and taking it to the cities. There it lay in great piles, like sand on the seashore, until people stopped measuring the quantity because it was now too vast to be measured.

Then came seven years of drought. The fruit withered on the trees, the sun burned the harvest in the fields. In many countries all over the world, there was a terrible famine. Joseph gave orders for the stores to be opened, and the people were able to buy the grain.

In these times of great hardship, Joseph's brothers also came to Egypt, where they had heard that there was still enough food for everyone. They went to see Joseph, who was now the second most powerful man in Egypt, respected and honored by all, and responsible for the distribution of food.
Joseph pretended not to recognize his brothers. First he wanted to test whether they had changed. He secretly put a silver cup in the bag of Benjamin, the youngest, and then accused him of theft. The other brothers knelt down before him and swore that Benjamin was innocent. One of the brothers even offered to go to prison in Benjamin's place.
Then Joseph could no longer keep his secret. With tears in his eyes he told his brothers who he really was, and soon they all embraced, overjoyed at this reunion. Joseph invited his brothers and also Jacob, his father, to join him in Egypt.

Jacob was now old and tired. He let out a cry of astonishment and joy when suddenly he saw before him the son he had long since given up for dead. He flung his arms around Joseph's neck, weeping with happiness, and did not want to let him go. And so for a long time he held his youngest son tightly in his arms.

Joseph's eleven brothers bowed down to him, for he was now Pharaoh's second-in-command. "So you are the eleven stars from my dream!" said Joseph. "Do you remember? Many years ago I told you about it. In my dream, the sun, the moon, and eleven stars bowed down to me. Since then, many of my dreams have come true."

The seven years of drought that Joseph had seen in his dream had not yet passed. He looked for a piece of land to give to his father, his brothers, and their families, and he gave them so much bread that they and their children always had enough to eat.

Even after his father died, Joseph looked after his brothers. "We once did you wrong," said one of the brothers. "Will you ever be able to forgive us?"

"Do not be afraid," said Joseph. "I forgave you a long time ago. You had bad intentions, but God made something good come out of them, by bringing me here. I shall go on looking after you and your children."

Joseph kept his promise. He lived to the age of one hundred and ten, and he remained close to his brothers right to the very end.

# THE BIRTH AND RESCUE OF MOSES

THE DESCENDANTS OF JACOB, Joseph, and his brothers remained in Egypt. Many years went by. A new king came to the throne, and he said, "We must be wary. The Israelites, who are foreigners in our land, are becoming more and more numerous. They are taking over our country. We must do something to stop them from increasing still further. And so you must obey this command: when their women bring a girl into the world, let her live. But when it is a boy, he must be killed. We cannot allow these foreigners to become mightier than those of us who were born here."

A man and his wife—descendants of Jacob, Joseph, and their families—had a son at this time. The baby was beautiful and smiled at them, and they were full of joy. But after the new Pharaoh had issued his terrible order, they feared for their son's life.

For three months the parents hid their newborn son in their house, but then their fear became too great. The woman took a basket of straw and sealed it with pitch and tar so that no water could get into it. Then she put the little boy in the basket and took it to the banks of the Nile. There, among the reeds, she carefully laid the little straw boat in the water, with the sleeping child inside.

"If we humans cannot do it, then may God protect you," said the woman tearfully, and she left the spot.

That very day, Pharaoh's daughter came to the Nile in order to bathe in its waters. She saw the straw basket, and when she opened it, she found a weeping child inside who gazed up at her with wide eyes.

"It's one of the Israelite children," she said. "I know what my father ordered, but I feel sorry for this child. I will make sure that he is well looked after."

She gently lifted the straw basket out of the water, with the child still inside, and carried it away.

Miriam, the little boy's older sister, had watched all these events from a hiding place. She went to Pharaoh's daughter and asked if she should go and fetch a nurse to suckle the baby. It was her own mother whom she had in mind. Pharaoh's daughter said yes, and so it came to pass that the mother who with such a heavy heart had laid her son among the reeds was now allowed to take him home in order to suckle him.

She thanked God for his protection, fed her son, cared for him, and never left his side. After a few years, as agreed, she took him back to Pharaoh's daughter.

"I pulled you out of the water," said the king's daughter, "and I look on you as my own son. I shall call you Moses."

*The infant Moses is in danger of being killed. However, as in the story of Joseph, we learn that he is rescued from this perilous situation and goes on to lead a nation. A suckling—one can hardly imagine anything more helpless or more deserving of protection—is saved so that later he can lead his people to freedom. From a Christian perspective, this is a theme directly relevant to the life of Jesus.*

*The journey that Moses has to undertake with the people of Israel is by no means easy. The exodus from Egypt—"Exodus" is another name for the second book of Moses—only takes place after massive resistance. In the course of the journey through the desert, God reveals himself and gives his chosen people ten commandments that will enable them to lead virtuous and successful lives.*

# THE EXODUS FROM EGYPT

MOSES BECAME THE LEADER of the Israelites in Egypt. But Pharaoh was still afraid of the foreigners in his country. He made them work for him as slaves, and taxed them heavily. Whatever they did, he looked on them with suspicion, and so their life in Egypt became more and more unbearable.

"I shall harden Pharaoh's heart," God said to Moses. "Then he will let you go. Indeed he will drive you out of his land."
God sent terrible plagues to make the whole country suffer. Then, to show his power, he told Moses to strike the waters of the Nile with a stick as Pharaoh looked on. Immediately, the water turned bloodred, all the fish died, and the water began to stink so much that people no longer dared to drink it. Pharaoh was shocked to see the power of the Israelites' God, but still he refused to let them go.

Then God sent down more plagues: flies and pests and vermin of all kinds appeared in great numbers, attacking people and animals; hail destroyed all the crops; diseases killed many animals. Swarms of locusts descended like dark clouds over the country and ate up whatever greenery had been spared from the hail, until the last blade of grass disappeared. Not one fruit was left hanging from the trees. The plague of locusts grew denser and denser. They covered the earth and the sky until everything was black.

Pharaoh went to see Moses. "Tell your God that it is enough!" he cried. Then God made the wind change direction, and the new westerly wind, like a mighty hand, swept the locusts away into the Red Sea. There was not a single locust left in the whole of Egypt.

But as soon as the danger had passed, Pharaoh forgot his fear. He still refused to let Moses and his people go free. Then, at God's command, Moses raised his hand and total darkness fell upon the land. For three days no one dared to leave his house. The Egyptians could not even see one another because the darkness was so black. Only where the Israelites lived was there light.

But still Pharaoh would not change his mind. Then in his anger God made every firstborn child in Egypt die, from the Pharaoh's own son to the son of the prisoner in jail. Once more Pharaoh sent for Moses.

"Leave the country now!" he cried to Moses. "Take your sheep, goats, and cattle with you, but go! Go away from here at once!"

And so six hundred thousand men, women, and children, together with their sheep, goats, and cattle, walked in an endless procession through the land. Moses led the people who had been entrusted to his care, and they traveled onward toward the Red Sea. And God sent an angel to guide them.

But no sooner had the Israelites left his country than Pharaoh changed his mind yet again. "We cannot let the foreigners go," he said to his advisers. "We need them to work for us. They are important to us. Arm the soldiers. We must force them to return!"

When the Israelites saw Pharaoh riding after them in his chariot at the head of his army, they were afraid. In front of them lay the sea. Moses stopped. "Lord, what shall we do?" he asked God.

"Stretch out your hand over the sea," said God. "The waters will part, and you will be able to walk on dry land through the sea. I shall once more harden the hearts of Pharaoh and his soldiers. They will follow you, and the sea will swallow them up. Behind you I shall make a column of water and fire to rise between you and the Egyptians. On their side it will be dark, but on your side the night will light up, and the angel that has guided you will guard the rear of your procession."

Moses did as God told him. He stretched his hand out over the sea, and a strong easterly wind blew the waves apart. Then Moses and his people were able to walk on dry land through the sea, while the water stood like two high walls on their right and on their left.

Pharaoh and his army came after them. All the soldiers, chariots, and horses rushed into the sea, but the tall column of fire and water caused great confusion among them. The wheels of their chariots got stuck.

God said to Moses, "Stretch out your hand over the sea again, to make the water flow back."
Moses stretched out his hand, and behind the Israelites the waters of the sea flowed together again. It covered the chariots and their riders, the soldiers and their weapons, until the whole of Pharaoh's army had disappeared beneath the waves.

Moses and his people finally reached the seashore safe and sound. By this miracle, God had finally helped them to escape from Egypt.

Miriam, Moses's sister, took hold of a little drum and began to sing and dance from sheer joy. All the women joined her, and together they sang a song in honor of God, who had saved them.

# ON MOUNT SINAI

THREE MONTHS AFTER the exodus from Egypt, Moses and his people reached the Sinai Desert. They set up camp at the foot of the mountain, and Moses climbed the mountain in order to commune with God.

"I have brought you safely through every danger, like an eagle guarding its young," God said to Moses. "Soon I shall appear to you as a great cloud, amid thunder and lightning. Everyone shall see that I am speaking to you and that I have chosen you out of all my people."

On the morning of the third day after their arrival, the sky suddenly grew dark. There was thunder and lightning, and a dark cloud covered the mountain. All the people came out of their tents and were awestruck. Many were afraid. Children hid behind their parents. Mount Sinai was covered in smoke. There was a loud sound of trumpets, and the whole mountain seemed to shake.

Moses spoke to God, and God answered in a voice just like the thunder.

Once more Moses climbed the mountain. "Take these tablets of stone," said God, "and listen now to the Ten Commandments that I have written on them. Take them to the people, to use as guidance throughout their lives."

And God said:
"I am your God. You shall have no gods other than me.
You must not make false idols and pray to them.
You must not misuse the name of God.
You must not work on the seventh day. That is a day of rest.
Respect your father and your mother.
You must not kill.
You must not commit adultery.
You must not steal.
You must not tell lies about your fellow humans.
You must not desire to have things that belong to someone else."

Moses listened to the Ten Commandments. Then he climbed down from Mount Sinai to rejoin his people. The people looked up at the dark cloud hanging over the mountain and said, "We are afraid of this God." Moses said, "Do not be afraid. God has come to test your love. He wants you to worship him. He has led us safely along many paths, and he will always protect us." Then Moses raised his voice: "These stone tablets in my hands contain God's Ten Commandments. Come to me, all of you, and I will show them to you. They are to be our guide for the rest of our lives."

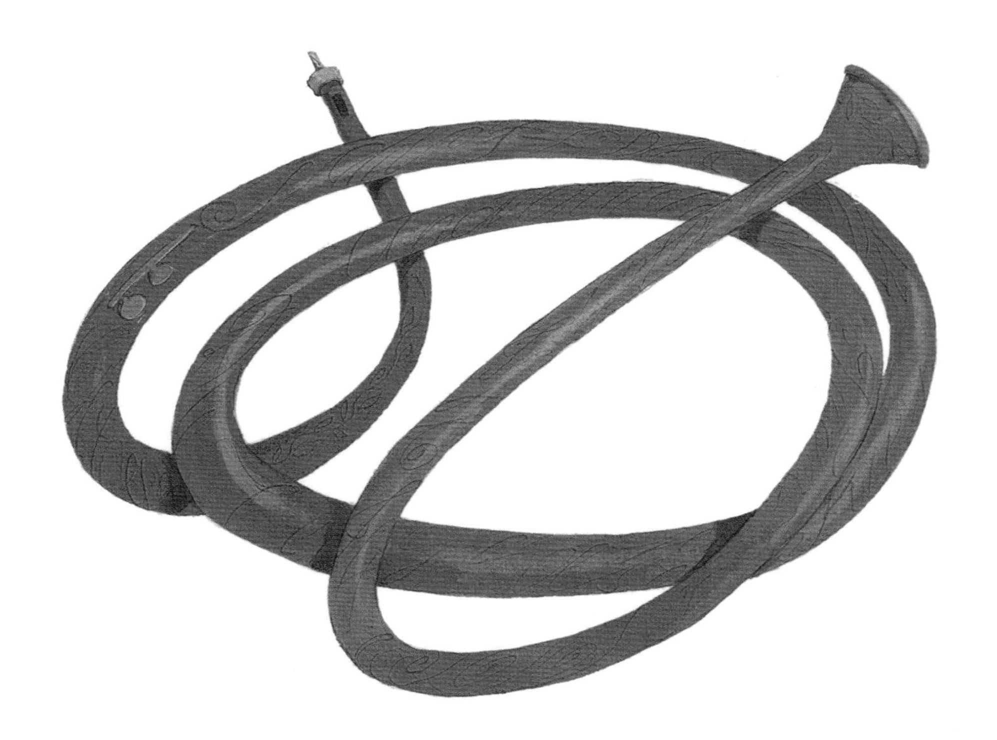

# DAVID AND GOLIATH

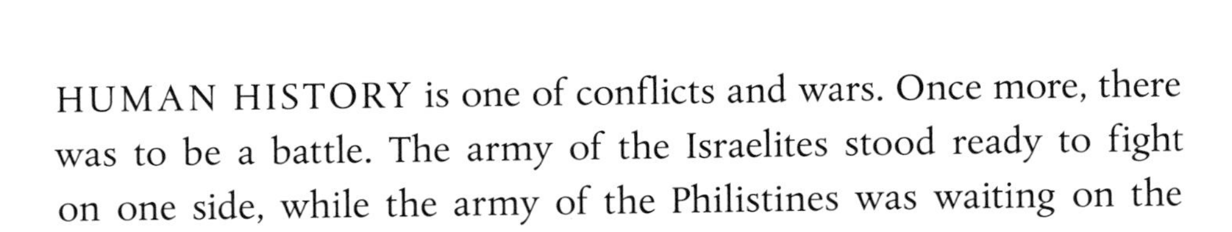

HUMAN HISTORY is one of conflicts and wars. Once more, there was to be a battle. The army of the Israelites stood ready to fight on one side, while the army of the Philistines was waiting on the other.
Then one of the Philistines, whose name was Goliath, stepped forward. He was over three meters tall, a giant who wore a helmet and a suit of bronze armor. In one hand he held a mighty sword, and in the other a spear with a shaft as thick as a tree trunk. Ahead of him walked a man carrying his shield.

"Why are you all preparing to do battle?" Goliath shouted to the army of his enemies. "Choose one man from among you, and let him fight me. If he beats me, we shall have lost. But if I win, you will have to become our servants."
Nobody dared to step forward and fight the giant. But then a shepherd boy named David, who was the youngest of eight brothers, approached Saul, King of the Israelites.

"I have to protect my sheep against lions and wild bears," he said. "I know how to defend myself. If I can fight lions and bears, I can also fight this giant!"

Saul was impressed by the boy's courage. He gave him his own heavy suit of armor to wear. "I can hardly walk in this," said David, and took the armor off. He picked up his shepherd's staff and his bag and said, "Don't worry, Your Majesty, God will help me."
David went to the riverbank and found five smooth stones, which he put into his bag. He had a sling in his hand. Then he walked toward Goliath.

The giant laughed. "You want to fight me?" He raised his sword, and walked toward David.
David started running, and as he ran he reached into his bag. He pulled out one of the stones, put it in his sling, and threw it with all his might. The stone struck the giant's forehead, just under the helmet. Goliath swayed for a moment, then collapsed to the ground. The battlefield suddenly fell silent.

Without a sword, and armed only with his sling and a stone, little David had conquered the giant Goliath. When the Philistines saw this, they ran away, and David the shepherd boy was cheered as if he were a king.

# ISAIAH'S CALLING

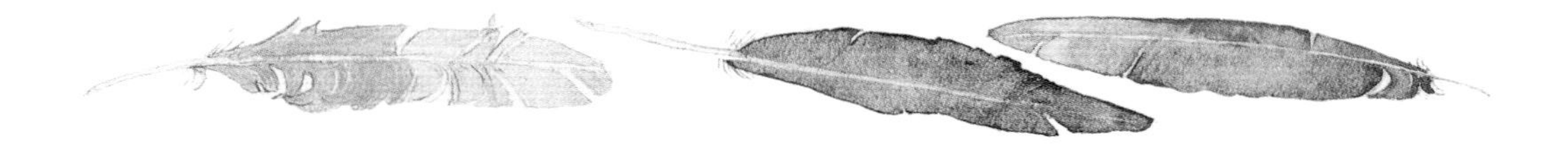

ISAIAH LIVED IN JERUSALEM. One morning—was it a dream?—he saw God sitting on a high throne, and the hem of his shining coat filled the whole temple. He was surrounded by mighty angels, each with six wings. One of the angels flew toward Isaiah, and in his hand was a pair of tongs that held a glowing piece of coal. He touched Isaiah's lips with the coal and said, "The coal has touched your lips. Now you are free from all sin."

Isaiah then heard the voice of God saying, "Who is prepared to be our messenger? Who can I send to speak to the people?"

Isaiah answered in a loud voice, "Send me. I will be your messenger."

And so Isaiah became a prophet with the task of reminding people to obey the word of God.

"People cannot see with their eyes or hear with their ears or understand with their reason," God said to Isaiah. "Hard times are coming, and they will not want to know what you will tell them. But do not let yourself be led astray. The earth is unsteady. Like a drunken man the earth is stumbling, swaying like a hut in the wind, and humans sway with it. The moon and the sun are ashamed and turn pale when they see what people are doing to other people and to the world. Much will be destroyed.

But a new age will dawn. Then a new life will be possible. People will end their quarrels. They will turn their swords into plowshares and their spears into knives to help them work in the vineyards. No nation will ever again attack another, and no one will ever again learn the trade of war. From the stump of the tree will grow new shoots and blossoms." These were the words of God, and Isaiah listened attentively.

"A light will shine that comes from God. He will be the King of Peace. The wolf will be the guest of the lamb, the panther will lie down beside the goat. The calf and the lion cub will grow up together, and cows will graze beside bears, and their young will do the same. The infant will play with the snake, and no one will ever again do wrong or harm to others."

Isaiah the prophet and messenger of God heard these words, and left the temple in order to tell the world what he had heard.

# NEW TESTAMENT

# THE BIRTH OF JESUS

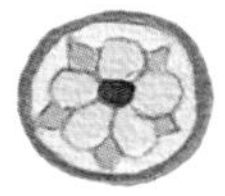

ONE DAY the air was filled with a dazzling light: God had sent the angel Gabriel to a young woman named Mary. She lived in a place called Nazareth, in Galilee. Mary was astonished at the light shining in her room, and was even more astonished to see the angel suddenly standing in front of her. She was startled, and her heart was beating wildly.

"Do not be afraid," said the angel. "The Lord is with you." Mary was also surprised by this strange greeting.

"What do you mean?" she asked softly.

Then the angel told her he had important news for her—news from God that would not only change her life, but also the lives of all the people on earth. Mary felt faint. What sort of news could this be?

"Do not be afraid," the angel said again. "God looks upon you with favor. You will become pregnant and will give birth to a son. You are to call him Jesus. He will be the son of God, and his rule will never end."

Mary felt her cheeks begin to burn. "I am engaged to be married to Joseph the carpenter. I am a virgin and I have never slept with a man," she said. "How, then, can I become pregnant?"

"Nothing is impossible for God," said the angel. "Trust in him. He can perform miracles. Are you ready for such a miracle?"

Mary was suddenly overcome by a deep and inexplicable feeling of peace. God had chosen her out of all the women in the world! She did not need to puzzle any more over the angel's message.

"I am ready," she said in a firm, clear voice.

Everything happened just as the angel had said it would. Mary became pregnant, and Joseph was by her side.

At this time, the Emperor Augustus ordered that a census should take place in his empire. Everyone must return to their hometown in order to be counted. And so Joseph and Mary left Nazareth in Galilee and set out for Bethlehem in Judea. It was a long and difficult journey.

Many people were traveling, and wherever they went they had to wait a long time for food and drink and also for a bed where they could spend the night.

Mary was now heavily pregnant. The journey had been particularly stressful for her, and she often needed to take a rest. Their progress was therefore very slow. Mary rode on a donkey, and Joseph walked beside her.

When they finally reached Bethlehem, it was dark. Joseph and Mary went from house to house, trying to find a place where they could sleep, but because of the census all the inns and guesthouses were full to overflowing.

Joseph was worried about his wife's condition, because the baby could come into the world at any moment. It was essential for them to find a place to stay.

After a long search, they found a stable where there was room for them to lie down and rest. The animals in the stable watched as the two strangers came through the door and sat down wearily on the ground. It was cold in the stable, and the wind blew through the cracked door. There was barely space for all of them, and the animals snuggled up close to the man and woman to give them warmth.

That night in the stable, Mary gave birth to a son. Joseph was at her side, and helped her through the birth. With tears of joy in his eyes, he showed Mary the newborn child, and they named him Jesus.
Mary wrapped the baby in cloths and laid him in a manger that she had lined with straw. The baby cried and looked at them with wide eyes. Then he fell asleep.

Mary and Joseph were filled with joy and gratitude. They stayed awake all night looking at the newborn child and watching over him as he slept.

While Joseph and Mary sat beside the crib in the stable, some shepherds were watching over their sheep in a field not far from Bethlehem. It was a special night, with many bright stars in the sky. Again and again, one of the shepherds would look up in astonishment. Suddenly the sky above them became even brighter, and an angel appeared before them. The shepherds shrank back because they were frightened.

"Do not be afraid," said the angel. "Something wonderful has happened, and you shall be the first to know about it. Tonight Jesus, the Son of God, was born. Go to Bethlehem. There you will find a child in a stable. It is lying in a manger lined with straw."
Then many more angels appeared. They praised God, and the sky was bright with their radiant light.

The shepherds were filled with a wondrous sense of happiness.
"Let's go to Bethlehem," said the oldest shepherd. "Let's welcome the child to the world."

One of the shepherds stayed with the sheep, and the others set out on their journey. It did not take them long to find the stable with Mary and Joseph and the baby in the crib, just as the angel had said.
The shepherds told Mary and Joseph about their encounter with the angel in the field, and stayed beside the crib for quite a long time. Then they returned to the fields, and reported to everyone what they had seen and heard.

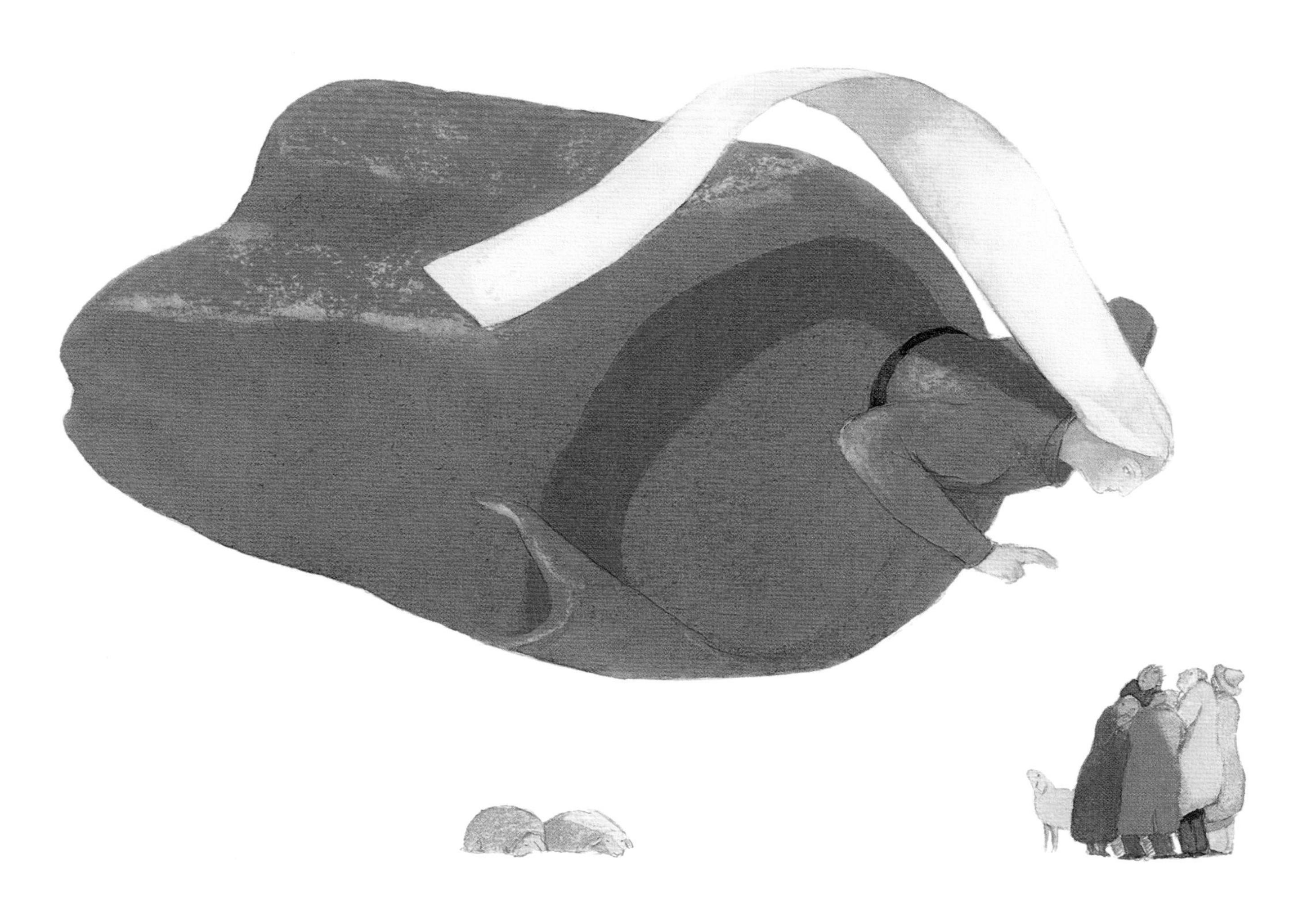

# THE ASTROLOGERS

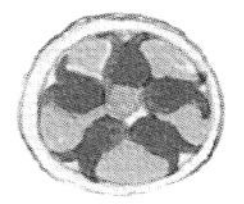

JESUS WAS BORN at the time when King Herod ruled the land of Judea. Soon after Jesus's birth, three astrologers came to Jerusalem from distant lands, asking, "Where can we find the newborn king? We saw a star shining in the sky, and it was so bright that it could only have been shining for a king. We have been following its light for many days and nights. Where is this king? We want to give him some presents."

When King Herod heard about the arrival of these strangers, he was afraid. A new king had been born? In his country? That could be dangerous for him.

He secretly summoned the three astrologers to his court and asked them when and where they had first seen the bright star. "Let me know when you find the child," he said, "so that I can also give him presents."

The three astrologers left Jerusalem. They looked for the star that they had followed across so many countries for such a long time. Impatiently they scanned the sky. Their camels restlessly pawed the sand with their hooves. Then suddenly, there it was: the great star, shining and sparkling as brightly as ever.

"It can't be much farther!" cried one of the three astrologers. They set out at once and followed the star, which seemed to be hurrying on ahead, as if to show them the way.

"We're expecting to see a king," said one of them, "so where will he be living? In a castle? In a fine house? In a desert oasis?"

The star guided the three men to Bethlehem. To their great surprise, it stopped above a humble stable.
"It must be here!" cried the excited astrologers, jumping down from their camels. They entered the stable. At first all they could see were the animals, but then they saw Mary and Joseph and the baby in the crib. The baby smiled at them.
Now they knew why the star had guided them to this place. They knelt before the baby in the crib and honored him as their king. Then they produced the gifts they had brought from their own countries: gold, incense, and myrrh.

That same night, God appeared to these three wise men in a dream. He told them not to go back to Herod. God knew that the king had something wicked in mind, and was afraid of losing his power. And so the next morning the three wisemen chose a different route to take them back to their homelands.

*The gospels of the New Testament begin with the birth of a child who enters the world in very troubled times. The child will become the savior of that world. He is the Son of God, and yet paradoxically he is born in a lowly stable, and his crib is a manger from which cattle eat. This symbolizes the fact that God is always on the side of those who are weak and deprived. And so the first persons to receive the message from the angels and to come and honor the child are some humble shepherds.*
*They are followed by the astrologers who had traveled from what were then believed to be the ends of the earth. This tells us that God's message of salvation is not just for the people of Israel but will spread far and wide throughout the world.*

# JESUS IN THE TEMPLE

JESUS GREW RAPIDLY, and he brought much joy into the lives of Mary and Joseph.

Once a year, to celebrate a special festival, they went on foot from Nazareth to Jerusalem, in order to go to the temple.

When Jesus was twelve years old, once again they went to Jerusalem to pray in the temple. There were many pilgrims in the city, including some of their friends and neighbors. And so Mary and Joseph were not worried when they set out for home again without the young Jesus.

"He'll probably be with our relatives in the next village, waiting for us," said Joseph. "We shall see him soon."

But when they reached their relatives' house after a long walk, and Jesus was not there, and none of their friends had seen him, they became very worried.

They quickly returned to Jerusalem. For three days they searched for Jesus in the crowded city, but they could not find him anywhere. Their fears for their son drove them with increasing urgency through the streets and alleyways.

Finally, their search led them back to the temple. They entered and then stood still in utter astonishment. In the midst of all the teachers and

high priests sat the twelve-year-old Jesus. He was listening attentively to all these wise men, asking them many questions and then responding to their answers.

Those who had come to the temple listened to what Jesus said to these learned men, and many were amazed at his wisdom. Mary and Joseph were relieved, but they were also upset.

"We've been looking for you everywhere! How could you run off like that?" they asked him. "We were so worried about you!"

Jesus embraced them. "You do not need to worry about me. God my father will protect me. And why would you look for me anywhere else but here? This is my father's house. Should I not be in the place where all thoughts turn to him?"

He stood up and followed Mary and Joseph, and together they returned to Nazareth. Mary and Joseph never forgot what had happened that day. As time went by, Jesus became wiser and wiser, and he was loved both by God and by his fellow humans.

*Even when he is just twelve years old, two things are already clear in the life of young Jesus: he is closer to God, his heavenly father, than to the members of the family in which he is growing up; and he is driven by the need not only to dwell in his "father's house" but also to follow God's will, even to the point of crucifixion.*
*This is the only story in the Bible that takes place during Jesus's childhood, and it already reveals his vocation. It is not long before he goes into action. He begins his work for God's kingdom by assembling a group of disciples. With them he travels the length and breadth of the land as an itinerant preacher.*

# THE FIRST DISCIPLES

ONE DAY, Jesus was standing on the shore of Lake Gennesaret. Many people were standing around him, because they wanted to hear him talk about God. Nobody could talk about God as Jesus could.

There were a lot of fishermen on the shore, cleaning their nets. They had spent the whole night trying in vain to catch some fish. Now they were tired and irritable.
Jesus went to one of them, whose name was Simon Peter, and said, "Take your boat out once more into the lake, and throw your nets into the water. This time you will make a good catch. Trust me."
The fishermen wondered at his words, and didn't really believe him.

Eventually, however, they went out once more in their boats and threw their nets into the water. They could scarcely believe their eyes. They caught so many fish that the nets were in danger of bursting. Simon Peter, John, James, and the other fishermen looked at Jesus with fear in their eyes. How could such a thing be possible?

"Do not be afraid," said Jesus. "Put your trust in God. Follow me. From now on you will be fishers of men, and you will tell everyone of the wonders God can perform."

The fishermen did not need long to make up their minds. They pulled their boats ashore, then left everything behind them.

From that day onward, they accompanied Jesus as his friends, companions, and disciples. Soon there were twelve disciples who were at Jesus's side wherever he went.

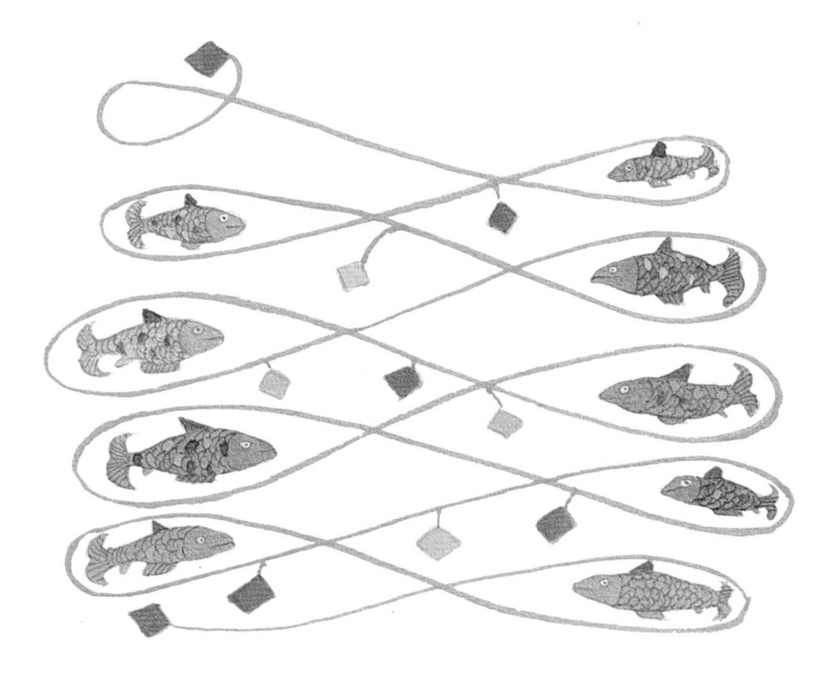

# THE WEDDING IN CANA

IN CANA, GALILEE, there was a wedding. Jesus and his disciples had been invited, and Jesus's mother, Mary, was also one of the guests. People danced and laughed and drank.

When there was no wine left, Mary said to Jesus, "They've run out of wine. And people want to carry on celebrating. So what should we do?"
Jesus looked around. There were six large, empty stone pots in the house. Each of them could hold almost a hundred liters. Jesus said to the servants of the house, "Fill these pots with water."
The servants filled the pots to the brim with water. "Take a sample of it to the man who is in charge of the food and drink," said Jesus. "Let him taste it."
The servants were puzzled by Jesus's strange command, but they took a sample to the man. He drank a few drops and looked at the servants in astonishment. The water had turned into wine!

"Go to the pots!" cried the man happily. "And fill people's glasses!"
The servants went to the pots and poured out the wine for the wedding guests. The bridegroom, bride, and all the guests raised their glasses and drank.

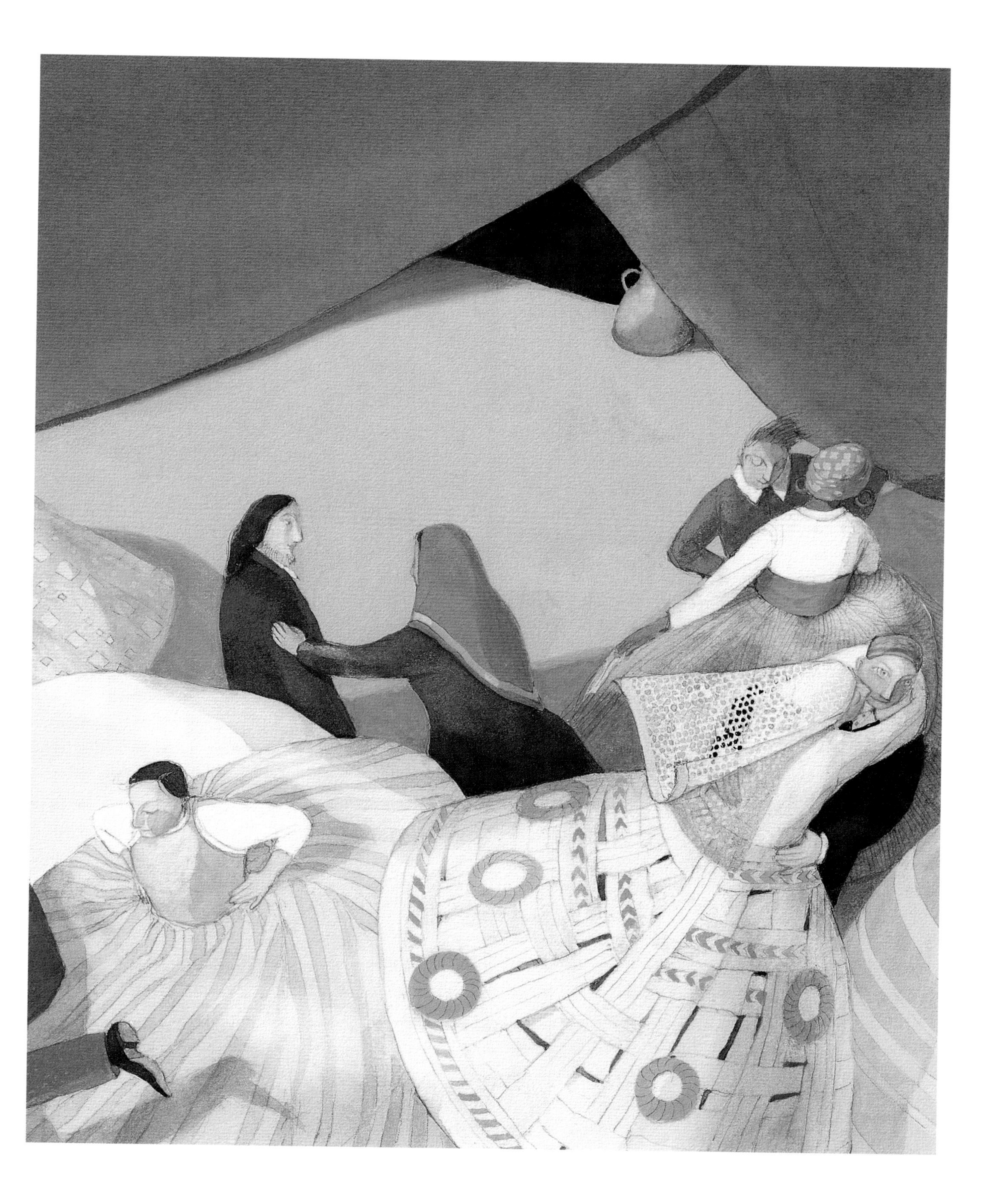

"You've saved the best wine till last!" one man said to the young couple. And everyone laughed.

But the disciples and those who had seen the miracle Jesus had performed were deeply impressed. This was the Son of God, for whom they had waited so long. The wedding feast lasted all night, and everyone danced with joy.

*The story of the wedding in Cana is the first report of Jesus's work in the Gospel according to John. The wedding feast may be seen as a symbol of the great feast that one day the human race will celebrate with God. By transforming ordinary water into delicious wine, Jesus is giving a clear sign: through a present shared with Jesus, God's promise of future loving care for humanity will be fulfilled.*

*The next story, in which Jesus heals a paralyzed man, sets this profound truth in sharp opposition to the claims of the scholars that they represent both wisdom and the law. This marks the beginning of Jesus's conflict with the theology of his time.*

# JESUS HEALS A PARALYZED MAN

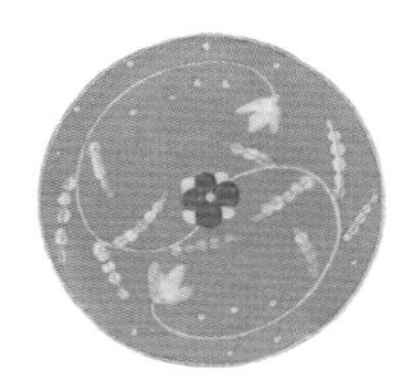

PEOPLE LOVED TO HEAR JESUS talking about God.
One day they had crowded into a house, listening to what he had to say. There was barely enough room for all those who wanted to see and hear him. Densely packed together, they sat or stood around him, hanging on his every word.

One of those who wanted to see Jesus was a man whose legs were paralyzed. He had heard about Jesus's wonderful work, and four friends had carried him to the house on a straw mat.
However, the entrance to the house was blocked by the crowd of people, and they could not get through. In desperation the four friends decided to carry the paralyzed man up onto the flat roof of the house.

But how would Jesus know they were there?
They thought about this for a moment and then made a hole in the roof, which was made of clay. Through this hole they lowered their friend down into the house.

Everyone was startled when suddenly the clay roof was torn open and a man on a straw mat was lowered down among them. They somehow made room for him.

Jesus welcomed the man with the paralyzed legs. He could see from the expression in the man's eyes that he was filled with faith, and so he said to him, "I forgive you your sins."
The scholars who were present looked at one another in surprise. What had Jesus said? Was this not blasphemy? Only God could forgive a person's sins! How could Jesus presume to do such a thing?
Jesus saw the disapproving looks of the scholars.
"You must understand that the Son of God has the power to forgive sins," he told them. Then he turned again to the man with the paralyzed legs.
"Stand up," he said. "Take your mat and walk."

Everyone fell silent. Had Jesus not seen that the man was paralyzed?
The man looked at Jesus with eyes full of gratitude. Then he slowly stood up from his mat, took it under his arm and, before the very eyes of all those present, walked out of the house.

The people who had come to see Jesus were astonished and delighted. They could not stop talking about the miracle they had witnessed, and it confirmed them in their faith.

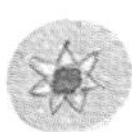

*Under the influence of religion, ancient society tended to exclude the poor and the sick, as well as children—who are the subject of the next chapter. The reason for this exclusion was that they were not in a position to conform to religious rules and regulations or fulfil religious requirements, such as fasting. Even the disciples tried to keep children away from Jesus. Jesus himself, however, simply reverses the social perspectives of his time and says, "Let us all be like children." What he is referring to here is the receptiveness that is characteristic of children. They have the incalculable advantage that their view of the world has not yet been distorted by prejudices and personal ambitions, and so they are open to whatever is offered to them.*

*To be "like children" actually means that people should no longer allow their fixed ideas and preconceptions to block their progress, but they should make their way through life with their senses and hearts wide open, prepared to see, hear, and feel the world around them.*

# JESUS AND THE CHILDREN

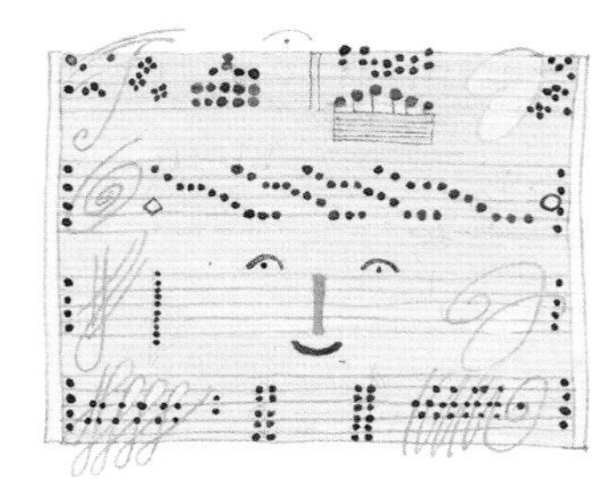

THERE WERE SOME MEN AND WOMEN who wanted to bring their children to see Jesus, but the disciples would not let them. When Jesus heard this, he was angry.

He called his disciples together and said, "Let the children come to me, no matter when or where. Never stop them, because for them God's doors are always open. Let us all be like children. I say to you that if your heart is not as open as that of a child, then there are many things you will never see. Children know the secret of life."

Then he went to the children, put his hands on them, and blessed them.

# THE GOOD SAMARITAN

A CLEVER MAN wanted to test Jesus. He asked, "What must I do to be given eternal life?"

Jesus said, "Is it not written in the scriptures? What have you read there?"

"That I must love and honor God," the man replied. "And that I should love my neighbor as I love myself."

"That is the right answer," said Jesus. "Do this, and you will lead a good life."

The man persisted. "But how am I to interpret that? Who is my neighbor?"

"I shall answer you with a story," said Jesus, and this is the story he told:

"A man was traveling from Jerusalem to Jericho. On the way, he encountered a gang of robbers. They attacked him, knocked him to the ground, and took all the belongings he had with him. Then they left him lying in the road.

"Soon another man passed that way. He was a priest. He was shocked to see the man lying in the road and stopped. Then he lowered his eyes in embarrassment, mumbled a few words, and hurried away without helping the injured man.

"Shortly afterward, another priest came by. He also stopped to look at the man lying in the road, thought for a moment, and swiftly went on his way.

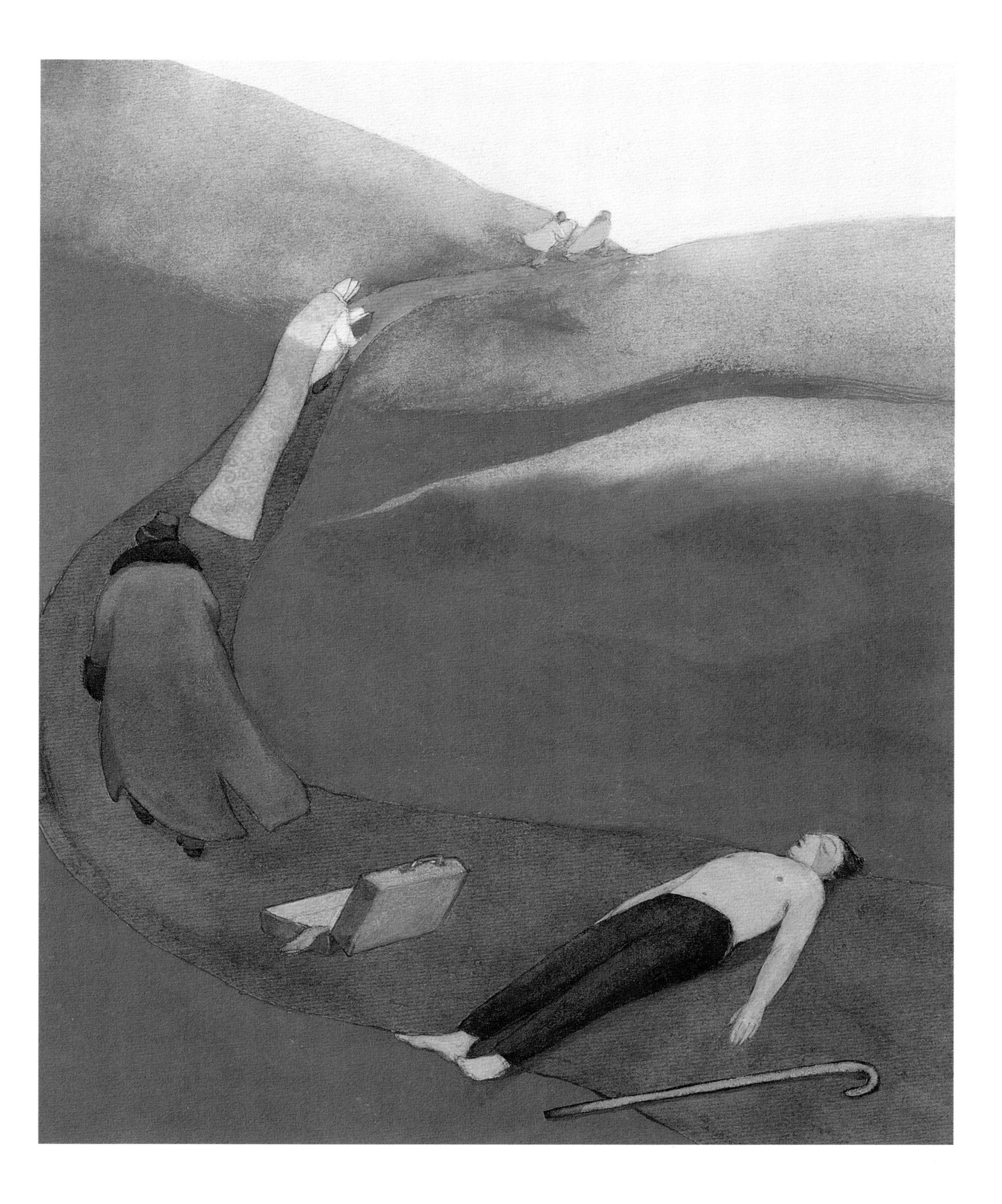

"Then a traveler from Samaria came along the road. When he saw the injured man, he stopped, knelt down, and bathed his wounds with oil and wine and bandaged them. He lifted the man onto the animal he had been riding and took him to a nearby inn. There he gave the innkeeper two pieces of silver and asked him to look after the victim.
'Take good care of him,' said the Samaritan. 'If you need more money, I will give it to you when I return in a few days' time.' "

Jesus smiled at the man who had listened attentively to the story of the good Samaritan. Then he asked, "Which of the three men do you think acted like a good neighbor?"
"The one who helped the injured man," came the reply.
Jesus nodded.
"That's right," he said. "Now go and do the same yourself."

*In the parable of the Good Samaritan Jesus once again turns conventional wisdom on its head. His starting point is the commandment to love and honor God, and to love your neighbor as you love yourself. A clever man asks Jesus, "Who is my neighbor?"*

*Jesus often tells parables. He does so because his main target is not the brain but the heart of his listeners. Here he tells a vivid tale in which two priests behave very badly, whereas the despised Samaritan from another faith proves to be the role model.*

*The story ends with Jesus asking which of the men acted like a good neighbor, thus making his listeners cast aside their narrow-minded self-centeredness and religious prejudices. In this way he invites them to see things through the eyes of other people.*

# THE SERMON ON THE MOUNT

MANY PEOPLE WERE NOW FOLLOWING JESUS. They had heard that he could change water into wine and had cured a man of his paralysis. Everyone was talking about the miracles he had performed.

When Jesus saw that more and more people were following him, he went up a nearby mountain. He sat down, and his disciples gathered around him, as did many other people. Then Jesus began to speak, and he used very simple, clear images.

"Each and every one of you is important," he said to all who had come to hear him. "You are the salt of the earth, which can never lose its flavor. You are the light of the world. Do not hide. With your light you can bring brightness to the world."

Jesus gazed at the people around him, and they looked at him expectantly.

"Do not be afraid. Good times will come for you. The sad will be comforted, the poor will become rich, and the peacemakers will show others the way."

Jesus took some pieces of silver out of his pocket and let them shine in the sun.

"What use to you are coins and other treasures? They will rust in time and lose their value, or thieves will try to take them from you. You will have no joy from them. It is better in the eyes of God to collect other

treasures, those that will remain forever in your hearts. Those that no one can ever steal from you. Are not a smile and a hug worth more than any coin?"

Jesus spoke for a long time up on the mountain, and for those who were listening, every word was precious.
"How can I see only the faults of others," Jesus asked, "and at the same time forget my own weaknesses? Stop condemning other people!"
He stood up. "There is one simple rule," he said. "Treat others as you would want them to treat you."

Jesus pointed to the mountain on which he was standing.
"Is it not better to build one's house on rock than on sand, so that it can resist the rain and the thunderstorm? It is the same with the words I speak. Whoever trusts in them will stand on firm ground. No storm can blow them away."
Jesus saw that all these people were hanging on to every word, and so he continued: "God is like a father. Have faith. Whoever asks for bread will be given bread, and whoever knocks at the door, it will be opened."

Then Jesus ended his sermon, and together with his disciples went down from the mountain.
All those who had heard him were deeply impressed, and his words echoed in their hearts long after he had departed.

*What is known as the Sermon on the Mount is the first of a great collection of Jesus's speeches to be found in the Gospel according to Matthew. His speeches and parables, together with his acts of healing and his miracles, are the main features of Jesus's recorded life. On his journeys they enable him to reach the hearts of many listeners, but they also arouse the displeasure of the self-proclaimed guardians of the law, the religious leaders of his time.*

*As in the Old Testament, the mountain represents a particular closeness to God and is the setting for divine revelation. Jesus's sermon is directed not only toward his disciples, but also to all those who are prepared to open their hearts to its radical message. But the very special mode of behavior that Jesus describes can only be accomplished through close proximity to God.*

# THE LAST SUPPER

THE FESTIVAL OF PASSOVER was being celebrated in the city. Jesus knew that he had made many enemies and that he was about to be arrested.

He asked two of his disciples to go into town and prepare a room for the meal. He wanted to have one last supper with them.

When evening came, Jesus and the twelve disciples went into town, where the feast was waiting for them on the top floor of a house. They sat on cushions at a long, low wooden table.

During the meal Jesus suddenly said, "I shall soon be arrested. One of you, who is even now dipping bread with me in the same bowl, is going to betray me."

The disciples were all very upset. Which one of them could possibly betray Jesus? They talked nervously among themselves. Then Jesus took a chunk of bread, broke it into small pieces, and gave one to each of them.

"Take it and eat it," he said. "This is my body."

Then he picked up a cup of wine, and passed it around among them.

"Take it and drink it," he said. "This is my blood."

He looked at each of them in turn.

"Do this in memory of me," he said softly.

The disciples ate the bread that Jesus had given them, and they drank the wine that he had passed around among them. They kept glancing sideways at him, for none of them dared to say a word. Was he really about to leave them? Who would be the one to betray him?

In every room of the house, people were eating and celebrating, and one could hear the clatter of plates and cups. The house was filled with the babble of voices.
Only in the room on the top floor, where Jesus and his disciples were having supper, was everything strangely silent. There was a heavy weight on the hearts of the disciples. It was sadness that made them silent. They knew that they would soon have to say goodbye.

# IN THE GARDEN OF GETHSEMANE

AFTER THEIR LAST SUPPER, Jesus took his disciples to a place called Gethsemane.

"Stay here," he said to them. "I would like to be alone in this garden for a while."

However, he took three of the disciples with him—Peter, James, and John.

"You can wait for me here under the trees," he said. "I shall go for a walk in the garden. The darkness all around, and the darkness that has suddenly entered my heart, make me afraid. I feel that my powers are leaving me. Do not give way to tiredness but stay awake."

Jesus walked away from the disciples. He was overcome with fear and doubt, and threw himself to the ground.

"I know that there are terrible times ahead of me," he said to God. "You can do anything. Can you not make this cup of bitterness pass me by so that I do not have to drink from it?"

He stood and looked up at the starry sky.

"What am I saying?" he cried. "Let everything be done according to your wishes, not mine."

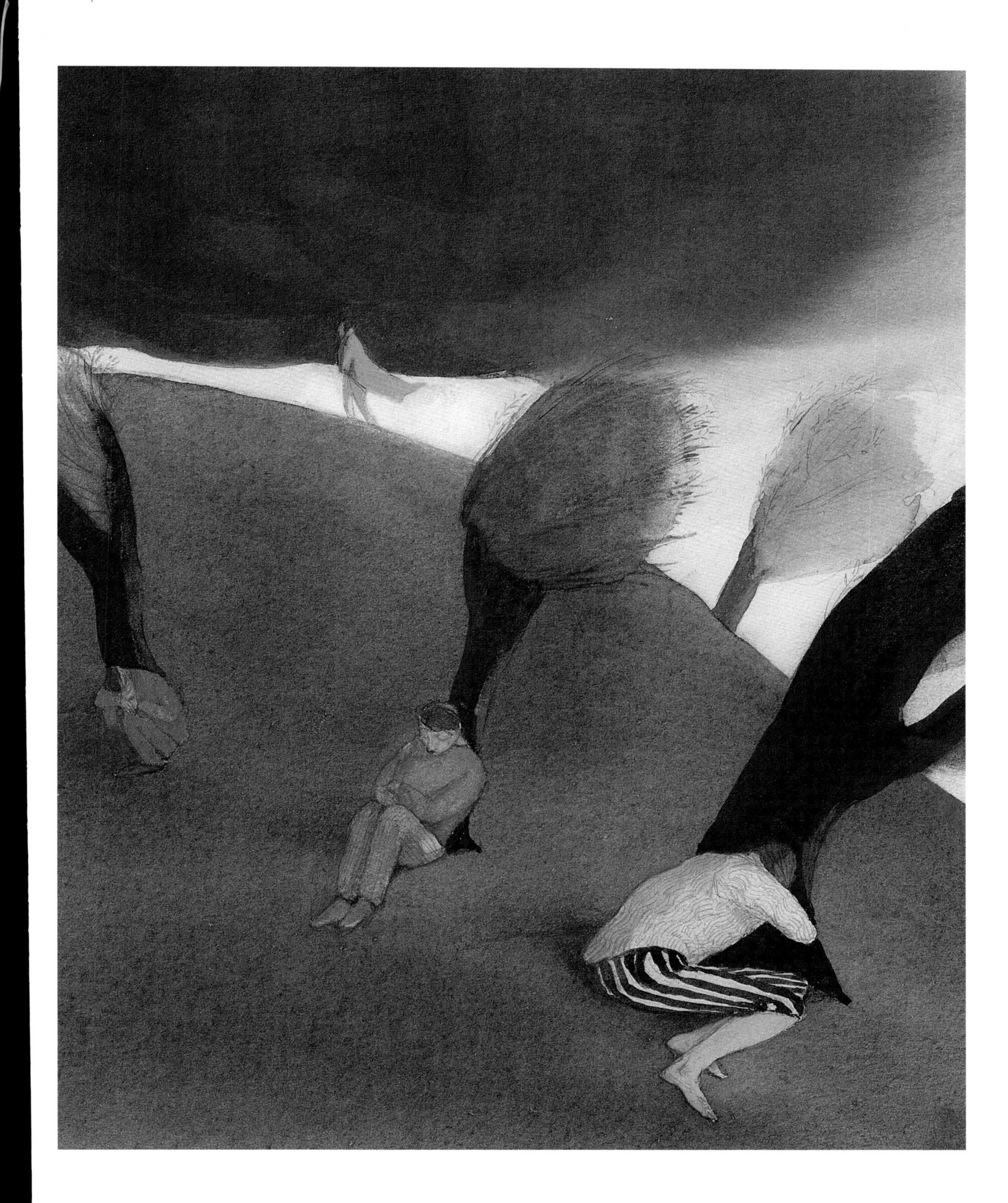

Jesus prayed to God to help him, then went back to join the three disciples. They had all fallen asleep. Jesus woke Peter. "You went to sleep? Could you not stay awake just one hour for me?"
Then he woke the other two. "I shall be back in a moment. I beg of you, stay awake and pray for me."

Jesus walked through the garden again, to talk once more to God. When he returned, the three disciples had fallen asleep again, worn out after their long day.
Jesus left them, and when he returned the third time, they were still asleep.

Jesus woke them up. "You have slept long enough. The hour has come. The one who will betray me is already on his way."
Even as he spoke, Judas—one of the twelve disciples—entered the garden. With him were some men who were armed with swords and clubs. Some of them were holding burning torches, which threw a ghostly light on their faces.
Judas went up to Jesus, kissed him on the cheek, and then stepped to one side.
Jesus allowed this to happen. He knew that Judas's kiss was the agreed-upon sign. Now the armed men knew which of these men was Jesus. They seized him and took him away.

Judas had been given thirty silver coins for betraying Jesus. Peter, James, and John trembled with fear and anger when they saw what was happening to Jesus. Then they fled into the darkness.

*Jesus sits for the last time eating and drinking with his disciples. During the meal, he takes the cup of wine that at such a feast was filled so full that it overflowed. Nobody was to drink from it because it was reserved for the Messiah, the savior sent and anointed by God himself. Jesus picks up the cup and hands it to his disciples so that they can all drink from it together.*

*This sign marks the beginning of Christ's Passion, the story of his sufferings and his death. In the Garden of Gethsemane, he tries to persuade his heavenly father to spare him from death by crucifixion, but finally he accepts that he must do God's will. At the foot of the cross, the officer in charge acknowledges that Jesus was the Messiah: "Truly, this man was the Son of God."*

# PETER DENIES KNOWING JESUS

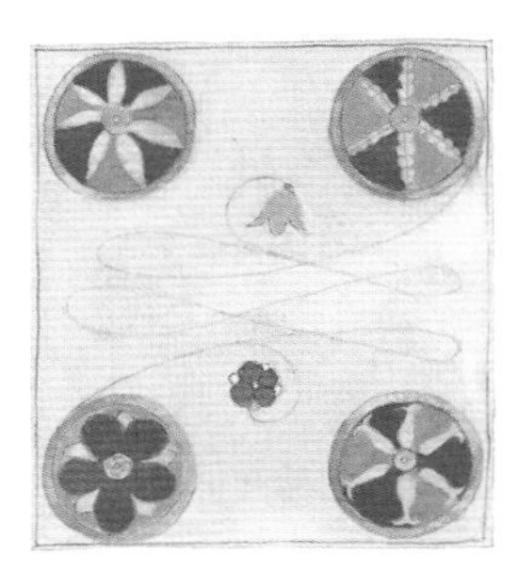

AFTER HIS ARREST, Jesus was brought before the Council of Priests in the temple.

"Are you the Son of God?" asked the high priest.

"I am," said Jesus.

This made all the priests very angry. They insulted Jesus and spat on him.

"You have heard for yourselves how he has insulted God!" shouted the high priest. "He thinks he is God's son. What is your verdict?"

Unanimously they declared that Jesus the blasphemer should be put to death.

Peter had secretly entered the grounds of the temple, and was sitting beside a smoldering fire in the courtyard. One of the high priest's servant girls passed by, looked at him, and stopped. "Weren't you with Jesus of Nazareth?" she asked. "Aren't you one of his disciples?"

Peter shook his head. "I don't know what you're talking about," he said. "I don't know this Jesus." Then he quickly turned his face away. At that moment a cock crowed.

The servant girl did not believe him. "He's also with Jesus!" she said to the people standing nearby. "He's one of the disciples."

Again Peter denied it.

When others also asked him if he was not a disciple of the Nazarene Jesus, who had just been condemned to death, Peter once more denied it.

At this moment, the cock crowed again. Then Peter remembered the words that Jesus had spoken to him: "Before the cock crows a second time, you will have denied three times that you know me."
Jesus had been right. Very slowly Peter left the courtyard of the temple. There were tears falling down his cheeks.

# JESUS DIES

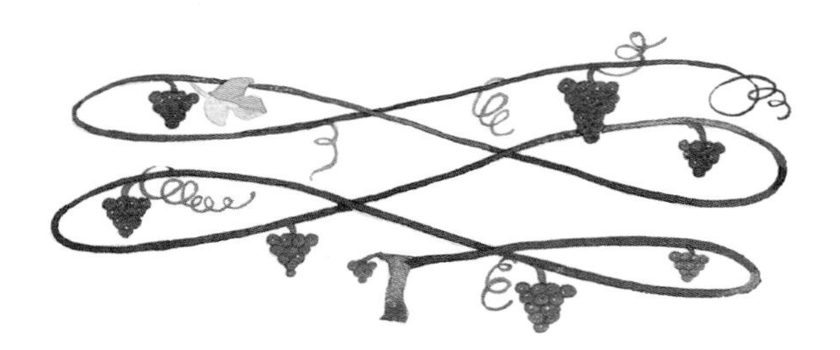

JESUS WAS TAKEN BEFORE PONTIUS PILATE, the Roman governor of Judea. The high priests accused Jesus of many crimes.

"Do you not wish to defend yourself?" asked Pilate.

Jesus did not say a word.

The Roman governor was surprised by this silence. He had already realized that the priests had only brought Jesus to him out of envy.

"Today I shall once again pardon an offender," Pilate said to the many people who had assembled outside his palace. "Should it be this self-proclaimed Messiah, the King of the Jews, or should I free another prisoner, the murderer Barabbas?"

The high priests had turned the people against Jesus, and so they all shouted, "Let Barabbas go!"

"And what should we do with Jesus?" asked Pilate.

"Crucify him!" shouted the angry crowd. "Take him to the cross, and let him die on the cross!"

Within the hour, Pilate had freed the murderer Barabbas.

The soldiers hung a purple cloak around Jesus, and they put a crown of thorns on his head. Then they mocked him and beat him.

"Long live the King of the Jews!" they shouted, laughing as they knelt before him.

Then they took the cloak off him and led him outside the town. There he was to be nailed to a large wooden cross, which in those days was the punishment for people who had been convicted of a crime. A man named Simon who happened to be passing by was made to carry the heavy cross for Jesus.

The soldiers took Jesus to a place called Golgotha. There he was laid down on the cross. With a stone hammer a soldier knocked nails through Jesus's hands and feet. Then the cross was pulled upright.

On Pilate's orders, another soldier had placed a sign above Jesus's head, which said: "Jesus of Nazareth, King of the Jews".

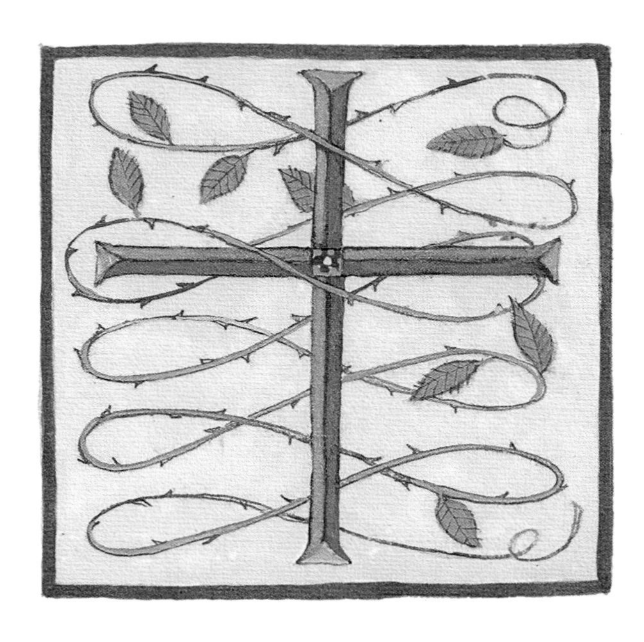

The people who passed by mocked Jesus.
"Are you not the Son of God? Then why don't you come down from the cross? Where are your miracles now?"
Even the other two crucified men on his right and left jeered at him.
"Why don't you help us? Where's your almighty God now?"
One soldier dipped a sponge in vinegar. He stuck it on a pole and pressed it against Jesus's lips. "Have a drink of that!" he said, and everyone laughed.

Jesus had been nailed to the cross at nine o'clock in the morning. At about midday, the sky darkened, and it remained dark for three hours. Then suddenly Jesus cried out in pain, "My God, my God, why have you forsaken me?"

There was a loud clap of thunder.
Jesus cried out again, and died.

At this moment, the curtain in the temple was ripped apart from top to bottom. The earth shook, and rocks split open.
The officer who was in charge of the soldiers and had seen Jesus die said, "Truly, this man was the Son of God."
Some women had also come. They had often heard Jesus talk about God. They had followed him on his journeys, and had looked after him. Now he had died before their very eyes. In deep mourning they stood before his cross. Dark clouds hid the sun.

# THE WOMEN AT THE TOMB

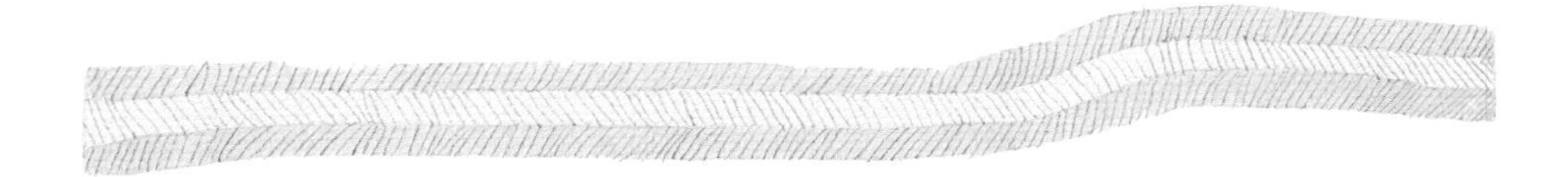

JESUS DIED ON A FRIDAY. That same evening, his body was taken down from the cross. A well-respected man named Joseph of Arimathea had been given permission by Pontius Pilate to do this.
He wrapped Jesus's body in white linen and carried it to a tomb that had been hollowed out of a rock. Then he rolled a heavy stone into the entrance in order to close the tomb.
The women who had followed Jesus to the cross came to see the tomb, and stood before it, grieving in silence.

On the Sunday after Jesus died, two women went back to the tomb. They had brought sweet-scented oils with them to put on Jesus's body. It was very early in the morning, and the sun had just risen, throwing a warm light over the land.
On the way, the women had wondered how they would get into the tomb. Who would roll away the heavy stone for them?

However, when they reached the tomb, they saw to their amazement that the stone had already been moved. Was someone else in the tomb? At this early hour?
The two women entered, and after a few steps they stopped in amazement. Were they dreaming? How could this be?

The tomb was empty. The body had disappeared.
Had Jesus been put in another grave? Had someone stolen the body? They looked at each other in disbelief. What should they do now?

Suddenly, two men appeared before them, moving as lightly as if they somehow hovered in the air. Their robes shone brightly and were as white as snow. The empty tomb was filled with their light. The two women lowered their eyes. They were frightened.
"Why are you looking for the living among the dead?" asked one of the men in a gentle voice. "The Son of God is no longer here. His father has awakened him from death. He died, and on the third day he rose again, as was prophesied in the scriptures."

The women were bewildered. Jesus had risen again, as had been prophesied? Could this really be true?
Now the second man spoke to them. "Go to the other women, and to the disciples as well. Tell them that Jesus has risen from the dead and they will soon see him."

The women curtsied to the two angels and then went to tell the other women and the disciples what they had seen. The women laughed and danced for joy.
The disciples, however, were full of doubt. Could this be true? Was Jesus really alive again? Peter hurried to the tomb.
He found it empty. There was only a white linen cloth lying on the ground. He gazed for a long time at the white cloth, and did not know what to believe.

*The tomb is empty. Jesus is no longer there. Once more it is angels, the messengers from heaven, who tell people the divine truth: Jesus lives—he has been resurrected. The two disciples who traveled with Jesus along the road to Emmaus have experienced his living presence within their bodies: "Was there not a flame burning in our hearts when he spoke to us on the way?"*

*After the Resurrection and the Ascension, the way was open for the birth of the Christian Church at Pentecost. Subsequently, Paul made many journeys all over the known world in order to spread the message of Jesus and the hope for the light that comes from God and brings peace to all humankind.*

# ON THE WAY TO EMMAUS

THAT SAME DAY, two of Jesus's disciples set out on the way to Emmaus, a village just a few kilometers from Jerusalem.
They walked quickly side by side, and the dust whirled up from beneath their feet. They paid very little attention to where they were going because they were so busy talking about what they had heard.
Peter and the women had found the tomb empty! Had Jesus really risen from the dead? And had he not prophesied that he would do just that?
But if he was alive, where was he now?
When and where would they be able to see him?
They were in a state of great confusion. What a day it had been!

Suddenly, a man appeared and joined them as they walked. It was Jesus, but they were both so deep in conversation that they did not recognize him.
"What's all the fuss about?" asked Jesus. "What's bothering you?"

One of the men sighed. "You must be the only person who hasn't heard about it. Jesus of Nazareth was crucified three days ago. We spent a lot of time with him, and often heard him talk about God and love. He had become a thorn in the side of the authorities, so they arrested him and nailed him to the cross. But now, three days after his death, they

are saying that the tomb is empty. Some women we know well—so we believe what they say—met two angels in the tomb. The angels said that Jesus had risen from the dead on the third day, as prophesied in the scriptures."
"'Why are you looking for the living among the dead?' That's what the angels asked the women," said the second disciple.

By now they had arrived in Emmaus, and it appeared that Jesus intended to go on.
"It's getting dark," said one of the disciples. "You seem to be a stranger to this region. Stay here with us. We'll be happy to share our supper with you."
Jesus accepted their invitation.

When they sat down at the table, Jesus picked up a piece of bread. He broke it into small pieces, blessed it, and handed it to them. Then it was as if the scales fell from their eyes. How could they have been so blind? Jesus had walked beside them and they had not recognized him. They jumped up from their chairs, but at that same moment Jesus disappeared.
"We saw him with our own eyes!" said one of the disciples. "Jesus is alive! Was there not a flame burning in our hearts when he spoke to us on the way?"

They immediately set out again to return to Jerusalem. There they met the other disciples and told them what had happened.
Even as they spoke, Jesus suddenly appeared again in their midst. "Peace be with you," he said.

Some of the disciples were afraid. Was this really Jesus? Or was it a spirit trying to deceive them?

Then Jesus showed them the wounds on his hands and feet. He ate and drank with them, and some of the disciples kept touching him, their faces filled with surprise and joy.

"You have witnessed everything that has happened," said Jesus. "Now go out into the world and tell the people what you have seen."

# JESUS ASCENDS TO HEAVEN

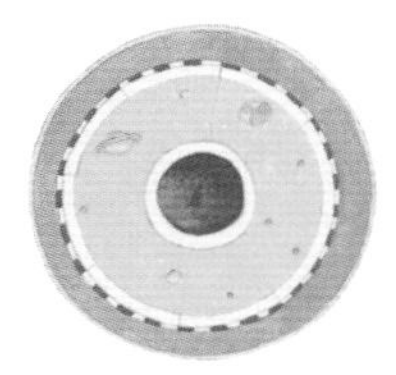

JESUS SAID GOODBYE to the disciples.

"I was once baptized with water," he said. "And soon you will be baptized with the spirit of God. The Holy Ghost will give you inspiration and strength. Then you will be able to travel the world as my witnesses and tell people about me. For I shall be in heaven, by my father's side."

Even as he spoke, Jesus rose into the air before their very eyes. Then he disappeared into a cloud that shone brightly in the sky high above them. As the disciples gazed upward, two men dressed in white appeared among them.

"Why are you looking up at the sky?" they asked the astonished disciples. "Jesus is as much here below as he is up above. He is with his father in heaven, and he is here beside you if you have eyes to see him. And whenever you need him, you will hear his voice if you have ears to hear. As he ascended to heaven, so too can he descend to earth."

The disciples told people all about Jesus and his resurrection, and many who listened to them asked to be baptized. Baptism was a sign of their commitment to Jesus.

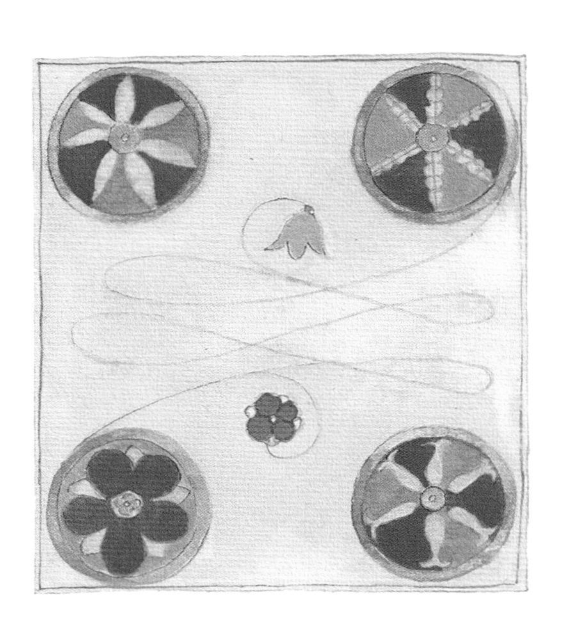

# PENTECOST

THE DISCIPLES and all those who felt close to Jesus had gathered together to celebrate Pentecost. Suddenly, the air was filled with a loud rushing noise, as if an invisible storm was about to break out in the sky. They all looked up in surprise. A bright fire was burning above the disciples and the others who had come to worship Jesus. The fire split up into small flames that flickered and danced above the heads of the men and women.

They could all sense the presence of God, and they began to talk in many languages, each of them in a different one. Then they crowded together in their confusion.

"How can this be?" they shouted. "The disciples and their friends speak our languages—they know all our mother tongues! And yet they have never left their own country! How is it possible? What does it mean?"

Then Peter stepped into their midst and raised his voice. He told the people all about Jesus—his deeds and miracles and his violent death on the cross.

"But not even death could keep hold of Jesus," Peter told the amazed crowd. "After three days, he rose again. His tomb was empty; I saw it for myself. And now he is among us, filling us with his holy spirit. And so we should dance and celebrate and praise him in many languages. Whoever trusts in him and lets himself be baptized in his name will be saved." Peter's words went deep into the hearts of many. Jesus had risen from the dead!

Thousands of people went to the disciples to be baptized. They shared bread with one another and were united in their prayers to God. And so, day by day, the community grew ever larger.

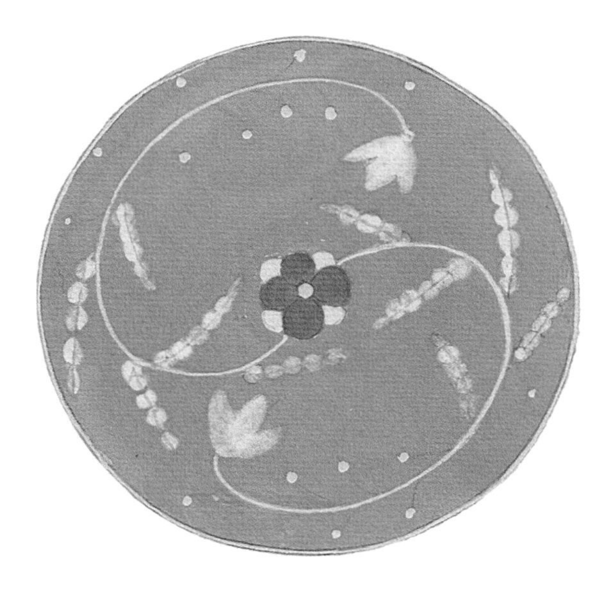

# PHILIP AND THE TRAVELER

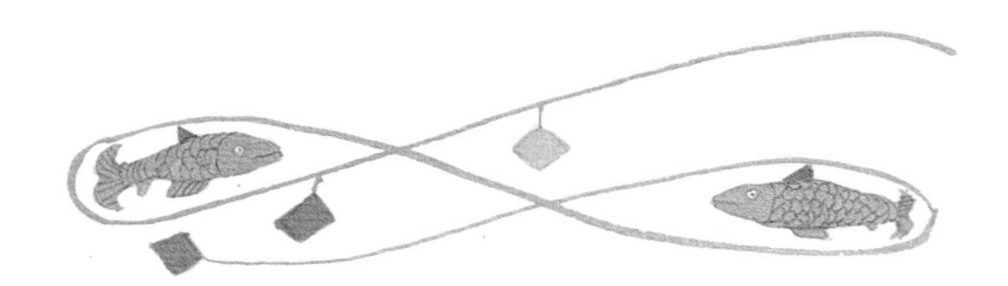

PHILIP WAS ONE of the disciples who traveled a great deal in order to spread the message about the resurrection and to perform baptisms. On one of his journeys he saw a chariot coming toward him. In it sat a foreigner who was obviously of high rank. He was treasurer to the queen of Ethiopia. He had heard about the mysterious Jesus and had come to find out more. He sat in his chariot reading passages from the Book of Isaiah.

"Do you understand what you are reading?" Philip asked him.

"How can I if there's no one to explain it all to me?" asked the man.

Philip joined the man in his chariot and explained the words of the prophet. He told the man about Jesus, his works, his death on the cross, and his resurrection.

"Jesus is still alive," said Philip. "We all saw him with our own eyes. And he is preparing a place for us in heaven. Many people are asking to be baptized in his name."

The traveler thought about what he had just been told. They came to a watering place, and he stopped the chariot.

"I feel a bond with this Jesus," he said. "Would you baptize me?"

Philip entered the water with the man and baptized him. But when the man turned around to speak to him, Philip had suddenly disappeared. "These are strange signs and wonders!" said the traveler in astonishment. Then he went on his way, rejoicing.

# PAUL'S JOURNEYS

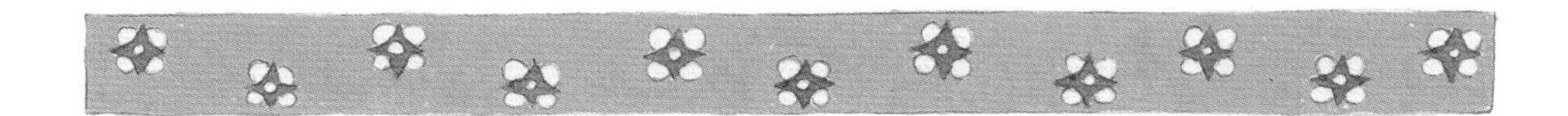

SAUL OF TARSUS was the leader of a group of soldiers, and he was greatly feared. He and his soldiers persecuted the men and women who spread the word about Jesus and the resurrection.
"This Jesus of Nazareth was a blasphemer!" said Saul. "And so anyone who spreads his teachings must be arrested."

One day, Saul and his men were on the road to Damascus. Suddenly, a bright light shone over the city and the countryside around it. The light became ever stronger and blinded Saul. He fell to the ground.
"Saul, Saul, why are you persecuting me?" asked a voice. It seemed to come directly out of the bright ray of light. Saul could see nothing.
"Lord, who are you?" he asked in fear.
"I am the one you are persecuting," answered the voice. "I am Jesus. Stand up and go to the city. There you will be told what to do."

Saul's men had stopped, fearful of the bright light. They too had heard the voice. Saul rose from the ground and opened his eyes—but still he could not see. His men had to take him by the hand and guide him to the city.
For three days Saul remained blind. He could neither eat nor drink, such was his state after encountering the dazzling light and Jesus.

In Damascus lived a disciple named Ananias. Jesus sent him to see Saul. "Jesus wishes to open your eyes," said Ananias, and laid his hands on the blind man. Then Saul was able to see again.

That same day he asked to be baptized. And then Saul, who had gone around arresting all those who followed Jesus, became Paul, himself a disciple who undertook many journeys in order to convert others to the Christian faith.

One day, Paul visited Greece and went to the capital, Athens.
Everywhere he saw stone statues of gods. The people worshipped many different gods. So would there be room for Paul's God among them?
On one sculpture he read the inscription: For an unknown god.
Paul stood among the people and said: "I can tell you about this unknown god who is to be worshipped here."
Then he told them about Jesus, his crucifixion and resurrection, and the miraculous conversion that he himself had undergone.
Soon there was a large crowd of men and women listening to him, and many of them embraced the new faith.

# THE GATES WILL BE OPEN

WHAT WILL THE CITY of cities, the City of God, look like? John saw it in a dream, and described it as follows:

"The city of cities will be light and bright and vast.
It will be surrounded by a wall, and angels will guard its gates.
The streets will be made of gold as transparent as glass. There will be no temple, because God himself is the temple.
The kings of this earth will take their treasures to the city.
And there flows the river of the water of life. It sparkles like crystal.
This river flows along the center of the city's main street. Those who are thirsty can drink from it, and will be given the water of life.
On both sides of the river grow trees that stem from the Tree of Life in Paradise. Twelve times a year they will bear fruit, and their leaves will be medicines for the people of all nations.

The gates of the city will always be open. They will never close, because there will no longer be night or darkness. The city of cities does not need the sun or the moon, for God himself is the light.
In the light of God's city, all nations will live in peace."

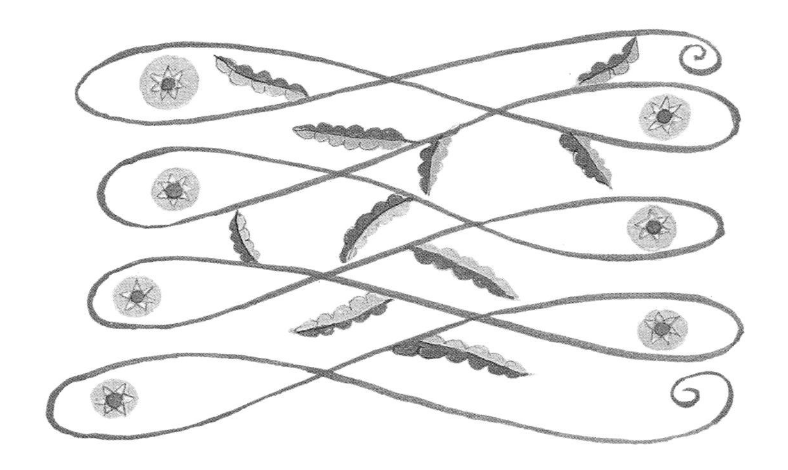

THE STORIES RETOLD HERE ARE BASED ON THE FOLLOWING PASSAGES IN THE BIBLE:

## OLD TESTAMENT

| | |
|---|---|
| The Creation of the World | 1 Moses/Genesis, 1,1 – 2,4a |
| Paradise | 1 Moses/Genesis, 2,4b – 3, 24 |
| Cain and Abel | 1 Moses/Genesis 4,1 – 16 |
| The Great Flood | 1 Moses/Genesis 6,5 – 9,17 |
| The Tower of Babel | 1 Moses/Genesis 11,1-9 |
| Joseph and his Brothers | 1 Moses/Genesis 37,1-35 |
| Pharaoh's Dream | 1 Moses/Genesis 39,1 – 50,26 |
| The Birth and Rescue of Moses | 2 Moses/Exodus 1,1 – 2.10 |
| The Exodus from Egypt | 2 Moses/Exodus 3,1 – 15,21 |
| On Mount Sinai | 2 Moses/Exodus 19,1 – 20,21 |
| David and Goliath | 1. Samuel 17,1 – 54 |
| Isaiah's Calling | Isaiah, 6,1-10; 2,1-4; 9,1-6; 11,1-10 |

## NEW TESTAMENT

| | |
|---|---|
| The Birth of Jesus | Luke 2,1-20 |
| The Astrologers | Matthew 2,1-12 |
| Jesus in the Temple | Luke 2,41-52 |
| The First Disciples | Luke 5,1-11 |
| The Wedding in Cana | John 2,1-12 |
| Jesus Heals a Paralyzed Man | Mark 2,1-12 |
| Jesus and the Children | Mark 10,13-16 |
| The Good Samaritan | Luke 10, 25-37 |
| The Sermon on the Mount | Matthew 4,25-7,29 |
| The Last Supper | Mark 14,12-25 |
| In the Garden of Gethsemane | Mark 14,32-50 |

# AFTERWORD

The Bible is a reader or, to be more precise, a whole library. It offers many texts of different kinds, written between the second and the ninth century A.D. But the Bible is even more than that: it is a book of life. The experiences that have been recorded in it are derived from the lives of men, women, and children who knew that they were connected with God and who understood that their own existence was the result of God's will and benevolence. It is richly rewarding to read these ancient but ever modern texts and to let oneself be surprised by unexpected discoveries. The Bible tells us that God is a living being who cares for us humans, who showers us with gifts, and who wants us to live our lives responsibly and virtuously.

Heinz Janisch writes books both for children and for adults. He uses his intuition and imagination to narrate these biblical stories in a manner that is colourful, warm, and lively. As he tells them, the stories move us and stay with us. He observes all the events with his soul as well as with his mind's eye, and he uses language that finds its way directly to the heart.

"In the beginning was the Word, and the Word was with God." This sentence, which stands at the very beginning of the Gospel according to St. John, also stands at the beginning of Heinz Janisch's book. It precedes the story of the Creation, and thus sets all the biblical tales in the framework of God's grace, the focal point and fulfillment of which is Jesus Christ. But this surprising and illuminating literary device also achieves something else. It reinforces the first thing we learn about God at the beginning of the Bible: He speaks. He is the Word. He is communication. When God says "Let there be . . . ," for everything he brings to life, including ourselves, it means, You shall exist.

Heinz Janisch's beautifully retold versions not only bring these events to life, but they also enhance our understanding of the theology. For example, in the story of David and Goliath, we read that "David the shepherd boy was cheered as if he was a king." This sentence at the very end of the story makes us realize that the tale of David and Goliath is one of the three texts that tell us how David actually became king.

The outstanding quality of Lisbeth Zwerger's art has been recognized by many awards, not the least of which is the Hans Christian Andersen Award for her life's work. With her serene and dreamlike biblical illustrations, she opens our eyes to a hidden world—that of divine reality.

Sometimes we can see references to the history of art. For example, there is a reflection of the hand of God from Michelangelo's depiction of the Creation in the Sistine Chapel. And in the figure of the angel cloaked in fiery red who appears to the shepherds in the field, the hair turns into a banner.

Such banners are frequently to be seen in late medieval paintings in which the angel appears to Mary or to the shepherds. It generally bears the words "Ave Maria' or "Gloria." The picture in which the astrologers kneel before Mary and the infant Jesus bears more than a close resemblance to Max Ernst's *The Blessed Virgin Chastising the Infant Jesus before Three Witnesses: André Breton, Paul Éluard and the Painter.* Lisbeth Zwerger even uses the same colors and architectural features that we see in the urrealist's painting. He too was an artist who saw beneath the surface of this world.

There is a uniquely magical charm in the appearance of the angel who informs Mary about her forthcoming pregnancy and the birth of her child. His reverence for Mary is so great that he falls to his knees and takes off his halo before her as if it were a hat. It is a sign of heaven's respect for a woman who is to take on the responsibility of bearing a son, knowing that he will be called "Son of God." She also knows that no one will ever really understand where this Jesus has actually come from. But it has all long since been planned in heaven, the messenger tells her.

Lisbeth Zwerger's pictures are like dreams of a life such as God might have imagined for himself. Rooted completely and concretely in our earthly existence, at the same time they are light and ethereal, reaching upward to connect with the source of life.

This book is meant for the whole family, and those who acquire it will have in their hands a beautiful piece of the treasure we call the Bible. The word "bible" stems from the Greek *biblion*, which means "book," and this book created by Heinz Janisch and Lisbeth Zwerger gives us personal access to accounts of our own origin and goal. This is not an everyday experience, and we can take our time to enjoy it. And if, as we read the stories and gaze at the pictures, we can gain a sense of divine reality, then our lives will be enriched by a perspective that takes us far beyond ourselves. We will be drawn—even if only for a moment—away from our daily needs and will be invited into the presence of the eternal, a presence in which we know we shall find peace and love.

— *Mathias Jeschke*

HEINZ JANISCH was born in 1960 in Güssing, Austria. He studied German and advertising in Vienna and since 1982 has worked for Austrian radio. He is the editor of the series Menschenbilder (Portraits of People).
Heinz has published a wide range of works, including many books for children and young adults, which have been translated into more than twenty-five languages. He is particularly fond of writing poems and picture books, but has also written several plays for the theater.
He has won many awards for his writing, including the Austrian State Prize for Children's Lyric Poetry, the Austrian Prize for Children's and Youth Books, and the Bologna Ragazzi Award; and he has been nominated for the German Children's Literature Award.
Heinz Janisch lives with his family in Vienna and in Burgenland.

MATHIAS JESCHKE was born in 1963 in Lüneburg, Germany. He studied theology and now works as an editor for the German Bible Society in Stuttgart, where he is in charge of the program for children's and audio books. He has written several picture books and volumes of poetry, and has also edited a series of modern poetry books in the German language.

LISBETH ZWERGER was born in 1954 in Vienna, where she studied at the University of Applied Arts. She is internationally recognized as one of the finest illustrators of classic fairy tales and of texts from world literature.

Typical features of Lisbeth's art are a gentle but nonetheless effective humor in her characterization and a love of mystery and magic. This enables her pictures to add a new dimension to the enchantment of a story, as opposed to explaining it and thereby reducing its magical effect.

Lisbeth's numerous illustrated books have brought her many prestigious awards, including the Hamelin Pied Piper's Prize and The Hans Christian Andersen Award for her life's work.

English translation by David Henry Wilson.

First published in the United States, Great Britain, Canada, Australia, and New Zealand in 2016 by NorthSouth Books, Inc., an imprint of NordSüd Verlag AG, CH-8005 Zürich, Switzerland. Distributed in the United States by NorthSouth Books, Inc., New York 10016.



Project management: Andrea Naasan
Editing and theological advice: Mathias Jeschke
Cover design: Cornelia Federer

Designed by Behrend & Buchholz Hamburg, Germany

Printed in Lithuania by BALTO print, Vilnius, January 2016.

Library of Congress Cataloging-in-Publication Data is available.
ISBN: 978-0-7358-4244-1 (trade edition)
1 3 5 7 9 • 10 8 6 4 2
www.northsouth.com

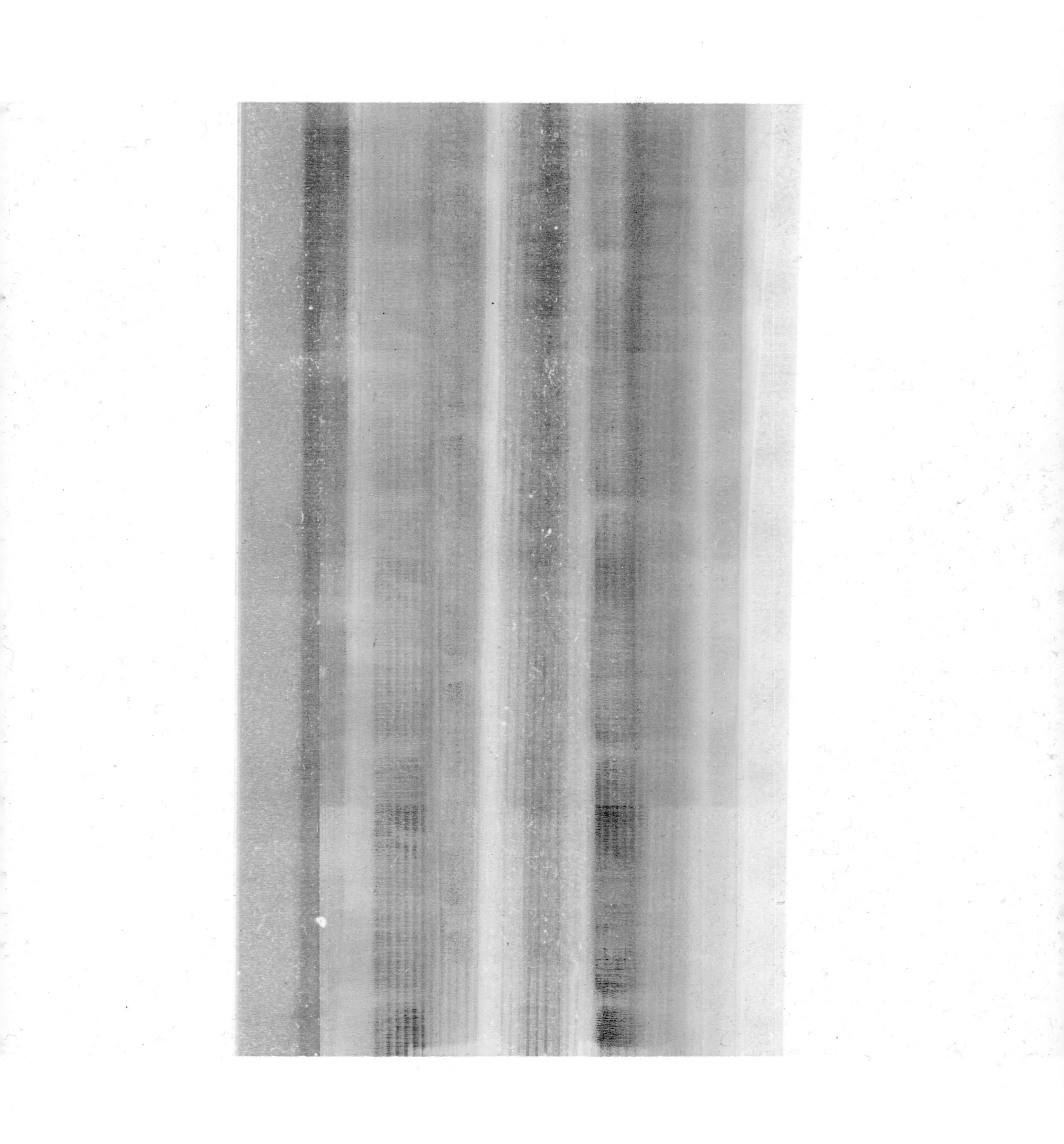